A Story of Strength

Lemanie Tomkins

www.ukbookpublishing.com
ISBN: 978-1-918077-35-3

Introduction

My name is Lemanie and this is my second mental health poetry book. After my first book was published I knew I didn't want that to be the last, as I still feel I have so much more to share with the world. This book is a story of strength, and rather than just looking at the dark side of mental health, I want to share the positive outlook I have had on life in the darkest of times. Although suffering with mental health has its challenges, I have learned so many important life lessons throughout my journey. My experiences with mental health is my truth that I wish to share with the world.

The beach

Three times a week, I am allowed to go to the beach.
A place where I feel so much at peace.
As I watch the waves come into the shore,
Seeing the seagulls that forever soar.
My little log as I call it, which is where I like to sit.
And it is my happy place, I must admit.
I got so lucky that I got admitted to a hospital so close to the beach.
It often helps me more than someone's speech.
I watch the citizens walk their dogs,
No matter the weather, sunny, rainy or fog.
Looking at the beautiful horizon where the sea and sky meet.
When I am at the beach I feel complete.
Only a five-minute walk from the hospital reception.
I know exactly where I'm going, the same direction.
As I stumble through the stones and sand,
I find myself at my log and I feel grand.
My happy place is the beach,
And I embrace this three times a week.

Your thoughts and feelings won't kill you

Someone once told me something that really stuck with me,
And I had never thought about it, but I really did agree.
And it is that 'your thoughts and feelings can't kill you',
And I never really believed that statement to be true.
Until I really thought about it, your thoughts and feelings can't kill.
All they can really do is make you ill.
The only way your thoughts can kill you is if you act.
And I know it's hard not to, but you don't have to react.
Yes, they cause an unbearable pain that you just can't explain,
And you just want to stop these feelings from entering your brain.
But they cannot kill you, they cannot take your life away from you.
And I know you might think suicide is the only
way out of this, but that is not true.
People take their lives every day, and it is
one of the leading causes of death.
I have tried myself and I know what it feels like,
as if you're about to take your last breath.
Suicide is a permanent solution to a temporary
problem, things won't always be this way.
So instead of ending your life why not choose to stay.
I know how hard it is to fight, day in and day out,
feeling like there's no hope.
Having so many negative emotions, feelings
and thoughts that you feel you can't cope.
But always remember, although powerful
and strong, it is all in your mind.
And that's not me saying it's not real, that's me
saying it cannot hurt you is what you'll find.
This world can be cruel and often is the opposite of kind.
But you are the one in control of your life, everything else is behind.

You don't have to do the things that are inside your head,
You can choose to fight them off instead.
So why not stay, just one more day,
And those thoughts might just go away.

Setback

Nothing hurts more than trying to achieve your dreams.
And you experience a setback of some sort.
And it makes you feel so down and distraught.
And it makes you question if this is all worth it,
Because you've just been rejected.
So maybe I should just go ahead and quit?
But this setback wasn't something I expected.
But it's a harsh lesson in life that things will set you back.
But that isn't an excuse to give up.
And it doesn't give you a reason to slack.
Instead you should do the opposite.
And go at it even more determined and even stronger.
Don't let this setback be the end.
And who knows it might take you a little longer.
But don't give up because something
bigger could be around the bend
And you won't know if you decide to let this dream end.
Not everyone is going to support you or
even agree with your dreams.
But that doesn't mean you should lose hope.
Even if you feel you can no longer cope.
It hurts when people put you down.
And it really does make you frown.
And it makes you wanna quit.
But then you're giving them what they want.
So go ahead and prove all those people wrong.
And try your utmost best to stay strong.
In my opinion the best type of revenge you
can get on someone, is success.
When they put you down and said you will make no progress.
You proved them wrong and showed them you can
achieve anything you put your mind to.
Because I can do it and I know it's true.

You will experience setbacks, you might
have people who think it's all a waste.
But those negative opinions can be replaced.
Replaced into positive ones, that make
you wanna show them that you can.
And you don't need their approval anyway.
Because it's you, you're doing it for at the end of the day.

I can't stand being judged anymore

When I finally think people are becoming more
understanding of mental health
Someone has to go and ruin my hope for this world.
I have heard every stigmatised phrase going.
And the amount of times I have been judged just keeps growing.
They tell me this is all just an attention seeking act.
But that is not true and when people say
that, it really does have an impact.
They tell me that I'm selfish for the things I've done.
But all I've done is try my best since my mental health issues begun.
They tell me I have nothing to be sad about
because I have a home, a family, and money.
But you can have everything in the world, and still suffer
with your mental health, this isn't even funny.
This is my life we are talking about.
When I constantly feel judged, I question why I should even stay.
Because you'll just tell me I'm overreacting anyway.
You'll tell me that other people have it worse than me.
But that doesn't mean I don't matter, just leave me be.
When I tell you that being in a mental health hospital is traumatic.
You'll say I'm lucky to be there and stop being so dramatic.
You will say I'm just lazy when I can't get out of bed.
Or you'll say I'm crazy when I have certain thoughts in my head.
The biggest trigger of mine is being judged every day.
It genuinely questions my need to stay.
And I know you probably think that's over the top.
But it's true because it feels like the judgement won't stop.
I think if people were more understanding
and kind this world would be a better place.
We wouldn't feel as if we have to
pretend we are fine and put on a brave face.

I would say the stigma is the hardest
thing about struggling with mental health.
Not the fact I feel so many negative emotions and don't feel myself.
The judgment makes our lives so much harder than they need to be.
All we want is support and understanding, so please leave us be.
Keep your opinions to yourself because they just make us feel worse.
The judgment and stigma we face feels like an evil curse.
We are still people at the end of the day.
And we are doing our utmost best to stay.

Recovery isn't linear

Recovery isn't linear is something I keep telling myself.
Because it is a constant struggle to try and battle mental health.
I think I expected to get better within a few days.
I thought this was just short term and even a phase.
But I was wrong, and I was very far from the truth.
Because I have been suffering with my mental health since my youth.
And I think the only way you can get
better is if you actively choose recovery.
And maybe I can encourage you through my words and poetry.
You can only get better if you really want to.
No one can choose recovery for you.
You might think you'll never get better.
While you're sitting there late at night writing your letter.
But if you have letters to write, you have reasons to stay.
And I believe no matter your situation, there is a way.
That is going to be a hard battle to fight.
But if you keep going I do believe you'll see the light.
Relapses may happen, and that's part of the recovery.
And if you keep picking yourself up you'll make a good discovery.
That you can do this, you can make it out alive.
And you might surprise yourself one day and even thrive.
I am going to fight and make a good life for myself.
And I might never go back to the person I was before,
but I can learn to live with my mental health.

If you have letters to write, you have reasons to stay

A saying that I love is "if you have letters to
write, you have reasons to stay"
What is meant by this, is that if you have suicide letters
to leave behind, you have reason to stay alive.
And I know it's hard to even think about that
when your demons won't go away.
And it is such a challenge to even get through the day.
And I'm not gonna tell you to live for other people because
you are the most important person in your life.
And I don't doubt you're in pain and you want it to end,
you can often just see the pain in someone's eyes.
But think about the people who you will leave behind.
Asking themselves is there anything different they
could have done to save you from your mind.
I have seen what losing a loved one to suicide does to people.
I don't doubt the pain mental illness gives you, it's lethal.
But ending your life and leaving loved
ones behind makes things worse.
Their whole world will come crashing down because
you're not there, and it will feel like an evil curse.
Some say suicide is selfish and I disagree.
It is not selfish to just want to be set free.
Be set free of their mind that right now is not being kind.
And all they want is to be at peace.
But their mental health has seriously declined.
You might not see a way out, and you feel things will never get better.
But suicide is a permanent solution to a temporary
problem, so don't even think about writing your letter.
People would rather listen to your story, than listen to your funeral.
And you might not think that's true while you're feeling so blue.
But your presence is worth so much more than you think.
And it's brave to speak out even if you feel like you're going to sink.

Some may say it is an act for attention and they think it's weak.
But that is far from the truth, it is brave to speak.
One conversation goes further than you realise.
I believe one conversation can save someone's life.
So don't suffer in silence, and speak up about how you feel.
And you will be heard because I know mental health is real.
So again, if you have letters to write, you have reason to stay.
And if you think no one would care anyway.
I'm telling you, someone would be sad you're not here.
Even if it's just one, your presence can brighten their year.
So before you make that split second decision that can end your life,
Why don't you think about this and put down that knife.
Your pain might end if you decide to leave.
But there will be so many people who will continue to grieve.
The pain doesn't stop when you die.
Because so many people will cry and cry.
The pain continues in others when you fly high.
The pain which you will leave behind when you die.
So if you're not quite ready to do it for yourself.
Do it for the ones who love you and would do
anything to save you from your mental health.
They don't want you to be a distant memory or a ghost.
They want you alive with them the most.
No one wants to grieve your death.
Knowing how you look at your very last breath.
As your family read your notes with tears coming down their face,
Knowing that they lost a beautiful soul that can never be replaced.
Wondering if they could have saved you in any way.
Maybe they could have convinced you to stay.
Once you make that decision you can never go back.
And suddenly everything goes black.
I have been there, I have tried many times.
And to be honest I still think about trying again sometimes.
But once I got very, very close.
And there was one thing I wanted the most.

I was laying on my bed in intensive care.
It was such a terrible feeling I couldn't bear.
And it was at this moment I begged the nurses to keep me alive.
Because I generally felt I was dying and I would not survive.
All this time I thought I wanted to die, but I was far from wrong.
It was only a near death experience that showed me I do belong.
I was extremely lucky as I survived and made a full recovery.
And I learnt my lesson and made a huge discovery.
That I in-fact do want to live, because
I really believed I was on my death-bed.
And the only thing I could think of is that I did not want to be dead.
So I fought with every breath feeling it would be my last.
Knowing that I had done something
so serious and now it's in the past.
But it almost cost me my life, I never thought I'd see the light again.
But here I am doing everything I can to get on the mend.
So if I've learned anything from my experience, it is not worth it.
And I almost did actually commit.
So I know every day feels like a never-ending fight.
But your future will be so bright.
Because despite your head telling you to do these things
You never gave in and you never gained your wings.
When your time is right I believe it will happen.
But don't take matters into your own
hands and make everything blacken.
So to end this poem, I want you to think
of a day where things are alright.
And although you wanted to, you didn't give up your fight.
So one day I truly believe things will get better.
And you'll be shocked that you ever
considered writing your suicide letter.

The ward

Being on the ward takes you away from the outside.
Losing all your freedom, dignity and pride.
Staff constantly checking, watching your every move.
I hope this admission will help me and I'll improve.
The constant screaming and shouting all day long.
And I'm trying my best to stay positive and be strong.
The banging you hear from people hitting their head against the wall.
Hearing the alarms go off when a patient presses the emergency call.
In therapy where you talk about your problems and why you're here.
Being on the ward was always my biggest fear.
Having groups where we all sit in a circle,
Talking about our issues and they say you should start a journal.
Fifteen girls, all with the same diagnosis living in the same space.
Sometimes we all get along, but other times it's a disgrace.
Wanting to leave but at the same time being scared.
Because you've almost forgotten what it's like to be
out in the real world and you're not prepared.
You want to go out into the community but
you're not sure how you'll function.
It could all go wrong and it could be a massive destruction.
You just want to live a normal life like all your friends.
Going to uni, having a job, going clubbing, the list never ends.
There are endless possibilities and opportunities waiting for you.
But it's so hard to think about the future when you're feeling so blue.
You start to lose touch with reality and the outside world.
Because you've been inside for so long and it's all kind of blurred.
You start to appreciate things a lot more like friends and family.
You just want to live a good life happily.
I never appreciated my life until everything was taken away.
A lot of decisions get made for you and you feel you don't get a say.
Knowing I can't just leave when I've had enough.
Being here is so difficult and tough.
People don't realise being on the ward is highly traumatic.
And I know you probably think I'm just being dramatic.

But you see and hear things that you were never meant to see.
You miss out on big events like birthdays,
Christmas and getting a degree.
Get put on all these meds, not sure if they're working.
You get no time alone as staff are always lurking.
You get told when to wake up, when to sleep, when to eat.
We do the same thing every day just on repeat.
Get given sedatives if you're distressed.
Although it may not seem like it, I am trying my utmost best.
The ward isn't a place I want to be.
But I hope one day, I will be set free.

Homesick

Do you remember when you would get homesick as a kid?
Maybe you went on a school trip, I know I definitely did.
I feel that same homesickness but as an adult.
No matter the age, if I'm away from home I'll get the same result.
I am almost 20 and I am far away from home.
And it hurts because being at home is all I've ever known.
I am in a psychiatric hospital hours away.
And I get homesick, just in a different way.
And I know a lot of people in the same boat feel the same.
But because we are full grown adults we may feel shame.
It hurts being back in the place I fought so hard to get out of.
It feels like a repetitive cycle I can't seem to break.
Ending back here feels like I've made a big mistake.
All I can think about is going back home to my family,
Because being away from them makes me feel so unhappy.
It truly breaks my heart to think we are apart.
Home to me isn't just about a physical building.
It can be a person or a place, someone's voice or a warm embrace.
I am working day and night to get back to where I belong.
I am trying my utmost best to keep going and stay strong.
But my stay here feels so long.
I need to be home with my family and I know I am not wrong.

What I needed, and what I got

When I started to suffer with my mental health
there were a lot of things I needed.
But I got the complete opposite in the way that I was treated.
I was faced with so much stigma, judgement
and a huge lack of understanding.
When what I really needed was support,
patience and more understanding.
The way the system treats those with mental illness is disgusting.
And it makes us mask and isolate and we become more untrusting.
It makes us feel like a problem or a burden.
And this just makes our mental health worsen.
There were so many things that I think could have helped me.
But instead I got judged for suffering and no one left me be.
I just get told I'm attention seeking and this is all fake.
I'm so done with the stigma I just need a break.
I get told I'm selfish for struggling.
And I have no reason to be sad.
But when you say these things to me, they just make me feel bad.
I get told I am impatient, demanding and I can't wait.
When all I want is help and support, not stigma and hate.
People with mental health issues need kindness,
compassion and care.
But we get treated like criminals and it is not fair.
Something needs to change, the system needs to change.
Because I feel a lot of the people who work
in mental health do it for the wage.
We need people who do the job because they want to help us.
Not who has a go at us every time we have
an incident and make a fuss.
To you we may be dramatic or over the top.
And we need this stigma and judgment to stop.

Because it only worsens our mental state.
And being faced with all this judgement doesn't make us feel great.
What I needed and what I got were two completely different things.
I can only hope that the future has something better to bring.

The spectrum

When you say don't beat around the bush.
I sit there and picture beating up a bush in my head.
But then you explain that's not what it actually meant.
And it actually means something else instead.
So don't beat around the bush means just get to the point.
But I have autism so I don't understand the phrases.
And sometimes it makes me feel dumb.
And sometimes I can't describe how I feel and I just feel numb.
You see the word spectrum is like a long, long line.
So you can be anywhere on the spectrum and that is completely fine.
Autism is a very wide condition.
As it has many different symptoms.
So people with autism don't speak at all.
And some people like me don't know when to stop and recall.
Sometimes I don't understand how people think or feel.
But to me my struggles are very real.
Social interactions can cause a lot of anxiety.
Which makes going out really difficult as
we feel we don't fit in with society.
I don't know when to join in a conversation and say my part.
I like to have a routine, almost like following a chart.
I find it hard to make friends and I often prefer to be alone.
Sometimes I want everyone to hear what I have to
say, but other times I want to be unknown.
Sometimes the way I speak may come across as blunt or rude.
And I don't know how to describe my mood.
I often talk over people and interrupt their conversations.
And sometimes I find it hard to understand basic information.
Autism is a spectrum, and it is a lifelong condition.
We are just like regular people at the end of the day.
Only our brains are wired in a different way.

They say

They say I'm crazy.
They say I'm just being lazy.
They say I'm attention seeking.
But how am I when all I am doing is speaking.
Speaking about my mental health.
And that right now I don't feel myself.
They say I have nothing to be sad about.
When they say that I want to scream, cry and shout.
Because I can't stand being judged.
When I am zoning, I need to be nudged.
But to you I'm just being dramatic.
I feel like such a burden and so problematic.
How can anyone bear to put up with me?
I'm scared they will see what I see.
A broken and unlovable person.
But these comments people make makes my mental health worsen.
You think I'm selfish for simply struggling.
But at the minute it feels like my problems just keep doubling.
I just want to be understood.
I want there to be a day where I actually feel good.
There is so much stigma around the topic
of mental health and it needs to end.
Because of the stigma many of us keep our
feelings to ourselves and pretend.

Normal life

Will I ever be able to live a life free of mental health?
Will I ever live to see a day where I sit there and think
you know what I feel a bit more like myself?
Will I ever live a life where my urges don't exist?
Will I ever be able to express my feelings without feeling dismissed?
Will I ever live a life where I don't need
to take medication to feel stable?
Will there be a day where my mental health
diagnosis doesn't feel like a bad label?
Will I ever be about to live a life outside of hospital admissions?
Will I ever be free of my mental health conditions?
Maybe I will never be 100% cured.
But setting realistic goals might help me feel more reassured.
Maybe it's about learning to manage rather than being freed.
Because our happiness isn't always guaranteed.
I just ask myself will I ever be able to go back.
Will I ever be able to get myself back on track?
Will I ever go back to the happy person I used to be?
Will I ever be able to get a job or even get a degree?
Will I ever be able to do things that everyone else can do?
Will I ever see a day where I'm not feeling so blue.
Will I ever is the question.
Will I ever overcome this depression?
I ask myself these things every single day.
I ask myself if there is a way.
And I won't know the answer to that question unless I ever get there.
But when I do find my answer I'll make everyone aware.
In the meantime, all I can do is have hope.
Even in the times I feel I can't cope.
Living a life with mental illness is the constant
question: will it ever get better?
Or maybe I should just end it and start writing my letter.
But no, I refuse to let my mental health win.
I will stay positive and take all of the stigma on the chin.

You might not see it now, but one day, things will change

I know what it's like to be in a dark, dark place.
And I know what it's like to feel as if you have to put on a brave face.

Feeling as if there is no future and you will achieve nothing.
But believe me one day you will achieve something.

Right now, you might not be able to see the light.
But one day, I believe things will be just alright.

It won't happen in a matter of days, it can take months,
years and a lifetime of fighting.
But don't give up because your story needs to keep writing.

You can overcome any battle life throws at you
and you can make it out the other side.
And if you don't do it the first time that's okay
Because at least you tried.

Life isn't always going to be easy but anything life
throws at you I believe you make it out alive.

And I believe one day things will be different and you will thrive.
And you will look back and say, I did it, no one did it for
me, but I did it and I made it through the other side.
And what you choose to do with your life now,
is whatever you decide.

When you're in a dark place it can be so hard to
see that things could ever be okay.
And you feel that this pain you're experiencing will never go away.

But please believe when I say things can and they will change
And at first it might be odd because you're so used to
suffering so it may feel strange.

But you are not your pain, you are not your
thoughts that are in your head.
So it might be hard to think about it, but try and look ahead.

If you can't see it now, that's okay, but one day you will.
And you might be in shock and just stand still.

And until things seem a little bit better, just keep going.
Sometimes that's all you can do, and you will keep growing.

All the tough things you go through
in life make you a stronger person.
And you might wonder what to do if things worsen.

And my answer to that, is just pick yourself up and try again.
That is the best thing you can do, go again and again and again.

Recovery isn't linear, relapses happen
but it's what you do after is what matters.
You pick yourself back up and climb up that ladder.

And never give up, keep going forward with determination.
And have hope no matter your situation.

Because like I said earlier, I truly believe me
and you can do anything we put our mind to.
And when you do it, you'll see life from a different view.

Absence makes the heart grow stronger

A quote that was told to me while I was in hospital
was absence makes the heart grow stronger.
I am hours away from home, for months on end, it feels
like my stay is just getting longer and longer.
When you are torn away from the ones you love it breaks your heart.
To know that right now I could be with them,
but instead we are apart.
But it makes my heart grow stronger,
because I realised what I am missing.
My family, my friends, my freedom, I miss living.
I never appreciated my loved ones until I was taken away.
And I can only hope that we will reunite someday.
Whether it's a matter of weeks, months, even years.
I will never stop fighting to get back to my family
and I will never stop shredding those tears.
Because without them I feel incomplete.
And when I miss them I can feel my heart skipping a beat.
Absence really does make the heart grow.
Because being away from my family makes me feel so low.
I never realised how much I loved and cared
for my family and friends.
And when I see them again will really depend on
when this hospital admission comes to an end.
But until then I will fight to be reunited.
And I will be so happy and excited.

Defeat the stigma

The stigma around mental health has to be defeated.
Because this is not the way we should be treated.
We should be treated with kindness, understanding and respect.
But instead we get judged and stigmatised and it is not correct.
Just because in your world mental health doesn't exist.
Doesn't mean for others it's just a myth.
Many of us battle every single day with our mental health.
Having to deal with low mood, urges, and just not feeling ourselves.
Yet to you we are doing it all for attention.
When in reality many of us are suffering from depression.
Or maybe some suffer from severe anxiety.
And they find it hard to go out into society.
Or maybe someone could have a personality disorder.
And we experience emotional dysregulation,
and we can't get our mood in order.
Some suffer from bipolar disorder which is where you
experience depression and manic episodes all the time.
But so many of you look at us and say "oh they're just fine".
Some people suffer from schizophrenia and psychosis
where you see and hear things that are not there.
But then they get treated like they are crazy and
what they really needed was care.
The list of mental health conditions goes on and on.
But the one thing we all have in common is the
stigma and judgement and it is not on.
Mental illness is often invisible and you may never be able to tell.
That someone is suffering and going through sheer hell.
Something has to change because this is not okay.
The stigma must be gone and things have to get better one day.
Because at the end of the day we're just like you.
And we want to be treated equally too.
Mental illness doesn't make us less of a person than you are.
We can still do great things in life and go far.
You sit there and judge us for the scars on our arm.

And then I try to explain that they are scars from self-harm.
But then you say why would you do such a thing.
Or maybe you ask me why I excessively drink.
I do these things to numb how I feel.
Because to me and many others mental illness is real.
I'm not saying what I do is right.
But it's what I do when I feel I can no longer fight.
And up until recently I've been taught no different ways to cope.
No different techniques for when I lose hope.
Some say I'm selfish and I only think of myself.
But that is far from the truth because I am
suffering with my mental health.
But that doesn't make me selfish and it doesn't mean I don't care.
Accusing me of that when I'm suffering is not fair.
I am just so caught up in my own struggles.
So it may seem I don't care but I have so
many emotions I'm trying to juggle.
People tell me I have everything, family, money, friends and a home.
But you can do absolutely everything in the world and still feel low.
You can have all those things and still get a disease like cancer.
So why is mental health different and why doesn't it matter?
I get so angry and frustrated with being treated so badly.
But this is the reality around mental health stigma sadly.
And sometimes it's not someone's words, it's their actions.
You can clearly tell they judge just by their reaction.
Not only is there stigma around mental health in general.
But men's mental health shouldn't be left untenable.
People say that when men are in pain and they decide to speak.
They are being childish and weak.
But gender is just a simple term that tears us apart.
But deep down we all have the same beating heart.
We all bleed the same colour.
And you can't just tell us to be tougher.
Men are humans too, they still have a mind.
Which sometimes can be unkind.

Men still have emotions, angry and mad.
Or maybe they feel anxious and sad.
What I'm trying to say is the stigma has to be broken.
And I will advocate for us for as long as I
live and refuse to remain unspoken.

Society needs to become more accepting

Society needs to become more accepting of invisible conditions.
Stuff like neurodivergent, mental illness and addictions.
People are so quick to judge yet they have no understanding.
But no matter what you say I'll still keep standing.
People can be so ignorant and small minded.
When what we really need is care and compassion provided.
Just because you can't see our condition doesn't mean it's not there.
So I am here to advocate and make people aware.
That there are invisible conditions that you may not be able to see.
And when I tell you they are just as important as
physical problems you may disagree.
But there is nothing harder than fighting a silent battle.
Having so many negative emotions makes the world rattle.
You just want support and understanding
from your family and friends.
But even those closest to you can judge and
sometimes it feels it never ends.
Even strangers on the street have approached me about my arms.
And then I have to try to explain that those scars are from self-harm.
And then they say "why would you do such thing?"
"Does not cutting your arm yourself sting?"
Or "why would you use a cigarette to burn?"
As they look at me with deep concern.
And I appreciate strangers caring.
But my scars are something that don't need sharing.
And I shouldn't have to explain myself to anyone.
Because right now it feels like my mental illness has already won.
I usually get two types of responses from the community.
One is genuinely worried and the others use this as an opportunity.
An opportunity to ask what you may ask?
An opportunity to judge and make me feel as if I have to mask.
It's so hard to carry on when you feel the whole world is against you.

So you start to hide and isolate because
you really believe it to be true.
I find people don't understand when they haven't even tried.
All we want is your support and for you to be on our side.
People don't like what they don't get.
But there are invisible conditions in case you forget.
Something has to change with society, family, friends,
strangers even those who claim they are trained.
Having all this stigma and judgement from so
many people makes me feel so drained.

There's always two sides

When it comes to being in a mental health hospital
it's always the bad things that you hear.
But I'm gonna tell you all the good things, like
there is always a staff member near.
No matter the time, day or night.
There is always someone around to help you fight.
Loads of groups so you're never bored.
There is always something to do on the ward.
Problem solving where we can all share our issues and relate.
We discuss anything you need and you're always
welcome no matter your mental state.
DBT where we learn skills every single week.
Then DBT skills review where we talk about
the skills we used and speak.
Therapy leaves where staff take us on walks down to the beach.
And if you're struggling or in distress there
is always staff within reach.
While there are a lot of negative things about being here.
And I can remember my first time I went to
a ward. I was filled with complete fear.
But I've learned to see that it's not all bad.
And one day you might actually feel glad.
Glad that you got that admission and you got the help you needed.
And you were able to move on and proceeded.
It's not all that bad being on the ward, there are good parts too.
There are so many resources to help you
when you need and help you get through.

When it don't just disappear

One thing I want people to understand more about mental health.
Is that no matter the time of year?
It's still okay for us to not feel ourselves.
Our mental illness doesn't just disappear.
Just because it's a certain time of year.
Or just because it's summer and the middle of May.
Doesn't mean we are automatically okay.
Even on events like birthdays and
Christmas people can still struggle.
It's not as simple as cheering up or having a bit of a chuckle.
Mental illness affects many of us every single day.
And just because to you it's a good time of year
doesn't mean our mental illness just goes away.
People think that we are automatically happy when it's a certain time.
They act like struggling on these occasions is a crime.
What I want to say is that our mental
illness can be there any time of year.
We can still feel emotions like sadness, anxiety, anger or fear.
This is something we have to fight day in and day out.
We can suffer at home, or at parties or when
we are simply just out and about.
From January to December and every month in between.
We want our mental health to be addressed and seen.
Because to you, you might think we have no reason to be sad.
But comments like these make me really mad.
So to end this poem I want to make one thing clear.
Our mental illness doesn't vanish just
because it's a certain time of year.

Success looks different for different people

Years ago success to me was about achieving good grades.
Now it's about getting rid of those blades.
Years ago success was about being the top of my class.
But now it's about getting these urges to pass.
Years ago success was about being in the top set.
Now it's about not burning myself with a cigarette.
Success years ago was about being
popular and being known as funny.
And having a good job and getting good money.
But now it's about being a happy bunny.
Three years ago I pictured my life being in
university and getting a degree.
Now it's all about being set free.
Being set free of what you ask, being set free of
my mental health so I don't have to mask.
I am twenty and I never pictured my life to be where it is now.
And I really want to get better but I don't know how.
I am sectioned and detained under the mental health act.
And three years ago I would never have believed that to be a fact.
My success is about getting better.
And to not think about writing my suicide letter.
Success to me now is about getting out of here.
Not necessarily having a job or a career.
Success to me now is about being free of self-harm.
And to have clear and clean arms.
Without any burn marks or any scars.
Not dreaming about being hit by cars.
Success to me is also publishing a book.
So people can take a deeper look.
Into what my life entails living with mental health.
And what it's like to not feel ourselves.
Writing poetry has helped in so many ways.

It's helped me get through so many dark days.
When I didn't know how to deal with what I was feeling.
But actually writing was the first step to healing.
So yes my success looks different from what I thought it would be.
My success right now isn't about completing a degree.
But that doesn't mean I can achieve.
Believe I can always believe.
Success looks different for different people and that is okay.
Because I know and I believe there will be a day.
Where I achieve something massive and I make myself proud.
And I may even be shocked and be wowed.
So right now my success is getting my book
published out for the world to read.
It's not what I planned, it's different, but it's still successful indeed.
It just looks a little different from what I had planned.
But I will not give up because I want people to understand.
What mental health is real and how much it matters.
And the stigma needs to be gone and people need to show manners.
My goal for my book is to help people feel less alone.
And to be encouraged to let their true self be shown.
Even if it shows suffering and pain.
Sometimes it's just caused by a chemical imbalance in the brain.
But I also aim to give people hope because as long
as you don't give up there is always hope.
So don't you dare think about hanging that rope, always
remember this in times when you can't cope.
Because you can achieve success, it might just look different.
But that doesn't mean it doesn't matter and it is and
always will be a massive, massive achievement.

Just bite the bullet, because one day you might just do it

There have been so many things in life I never believed I could do.
When people told me you can, I never believed that to be true.
Since the day I started writing poetry I have
always wanted to publish a book.
People would say "you should do it, why not have a look".
It took me months before I bit the bullet and decided to do it.
And to my surprise I did in-fact do it.
I surprised myself massively with what I could do.
And I believe the same can happen for you too.
Our head might tell us lies from time to time.
But that doesn't mean we have to listen to our mind.
Never in a million years did I think I could achieve this.
But why hold back and why resist.
You won't know if you don't try.
You need to do this and you need to apply.
Because when you achieve the things you've wanted for so long,
You will be so happy that you proved yourself wrong.
That sense of achievement I miss every day.
But that sense of achievement might now just look in a different way.
Before it was about getting good grades and going to uni.
Now it's about getting better and publishing
a book for the world to see.
I live for the day I can hold the book in my hand.
And I'll be so happy I'll feel grand.
Because I can look at it and say "I did this",
no one did it for me, but me.
Achievement doesn't have to be all about getting a degree.
So I'll say it again, just do it, just commit.
Because I didn't think I could, I must admit.
But in a few weeks my book will be published for the world to read.

And I am so happy I went for it and did proceed.
Because if I didn't I wouldn't be writing this poem right now.
So just do it, you might just surprise yourself
and make yourself go wow.

It's okay to cry

I want you to know it's always okay to cry.
Because even since birth it was a sign that you were alive.
It's okay to have tears coming out your eyes.
When you're trying your hardest to just survive.
Even if you cry and you wail and wail.
That is okay because that's what you needed.
You need to get it out and it does not mean you failed.
And crying does not mean you haven't succeeded.
It is a natural part of our everyday life.
So why should we feel ashamed?
Sometimes it feels like you've been stabbed in the back with a knife.
When all you wanted was not to be blamed.
Tears can roll down the side of your cheek.
They can roll and roll like a waterfall.
And it does not make you less of a person or weak.
And doesn't make you sensitive or small.
So let those tears roll and roll.
Until you feel a little bit better.
Because our mental health can really take a toll.
And I hope I can reach you through this letter.
Even when you cry, and you cry out loud.
And everyone can hear.
That is still okay because that is allowed.
But whoever you are please reach out to someone near.
You can cry and it can sound like a scream.
And it doesn't matter how loud it gets.
And it doesn't matter how extreme.
And when you cry please have no regrets.
Crying is part of life and it's how we realise how we feel.
So never feel ashamed for letting your emotions show.
Because this is you and this is real.
You're loved, you're cared about, and I just wanted to let you know.
That you can cry all day and all night.
And if I could I would sit with you and listen.

About how much you wanna give up your fight.
You can cry and cry if you don't need anyone's permission.
And this poem is also for all the men.
Men can cry and it does not make them weak.
And they can cry again and again.
And they are allowed to speak.
About how they feel and where their mental health is at.
Just because you're a man doesn't mean you can't cry.
And I will say that is a fact.
And that's something I want to imply.
So I stand for the women and the men and all the genders out there.
No matter your background, age or wealth.
I want you to know that people do care.
And it is so important to speak about your mental health.
So to bring this poem to an end.
Never ever feel ashamed to cry.
Reach out to a family member or a friend.
There is no need to be ashamed or be shy.

EUPD

Emotionally unstable personality disorder they call it.
One minute I can be fine and the next I can split.
Now you might be asking what does it mean to split.
And the best way I can describe it is it kind of
feels like you just want to quit.
Suddenly everything is divided and you
have very black and white thinking.
You can feel on top of the world and the next
minute you feel like you're sinking.
So many negative emotions I can't seem to translate.
Sadness, anger, shame, panic, loneliness, terror and hate.
Impulsive behaviour that can lead to serious danger.
But I don't think before I act, sometimes
I don't even know who I am,
I feel like a complete stranger.
My mood changes like the weather. One minute I feel on top
of the world and the next I feel like the world has ended.
I have intense but unstable relationships with others and
often push people away, but that's not what I intended.
Although labelled as a personality disorder
it is not my personality at all.
I want to be seen for me and me only, sometimes
I get so angry I just wanna hit a wall.
This diagnosis feels like a prison sentence at times.
The symptoms I experience often feel like a punishment to a crime.
Having EUPD feels like having all the mental
health conditions in one.
I wish this wasn't the way it had to be and I could just be done.
They say it's one of the hardest mental illnesses to treat.
And I'm scared I'll never be able to beat
this illness and feel complete.
They say people with EUPD are like people with
third degree burns over 90% of their body.
I just don't know who I am anymore, I feel like a nobody.

When it comes to being borderline.
They say there are nine main signs.
Impulsive behaviour like engaging in self-destructive activities
such as substance use, binge eating, or unsafe sex.
Emotionally unstable personality disorder
is a condition that is so complex.
Experiencing extreme emotional mood swings,
especially in response to minor things.
To you that trigger may be small but to me it really stings.
Having paranoid thoughts or feeling disconnected from reality.
I just want my life back, I want some normality.
Having a constantly shifting sense of self.
This condition really affects my mental health.
Having intense, short-lived relationships with family and friends.
To you it's not an issue but to me it feels
like the world is going to end.
Having difficulty controlling my anger and rage.
So many anger outbursts in which I engage.
Feeling lonely and empty even though I know people are there.
But no matter what anyone says or does
I always feel like no one cares.
Being abandoned when I need someone most is my biggest fear.
The symptoms of this condition can become very severe.
Last but not least, one of the hardest symptoms I suffer with
Is suicide attempts and self-harming behaviour.
I have attempted my life so many times and I can't even
succeed at that so I feel like a complete failure.
I have absolutely ruined my arms.
With cuts and cigarette burns from years of self-harm.
I look in the mirror and I look at my arms in complete disgust.
But then I did it at the end of the day so I need to adjust.
This poem may seem dark and like I am asking for sympathy.
But that is not the case at all, I am only raising
awareness for a condition that truly affects me.

You can't make everyone happy

If there's one thing I've learned in life, it's
that you can't make everyone happy.
No matter what you do, no matter how hard you try,
someone will always find a reason to be unhappy.
I feel I have become a bit of a people pleaser.
Yet people still find ways to be meaner and meaner.
No matter what you say, no matter what you do.
Someone will always find a reason to be unhappy with you.
No matter what job you have, or how much you make.
Someone will always find a way to point out your mistakes.
Sometimes it feels like whatever I do it's never enough.
And it makes me feel physically sick and rough.
I can't stand the thought of people being upset with me.
I can't stand the thought of people being disappointed
that I haven't got a degree.
But I suffer with my mental health, you see.
And it affects me every single day.
I struggle to see a time where things are okay.
And I can't meet everyone's expectations.
I can't please them no matter the situation.
I feel people look down on me because I don't have a job.
And it truly does make me want to sob.
I don't want to be a disappointment to my family and friends.
I don't want to be seen as the one who's achieved nothing in the end.
I don't want to be compared to people around me.
Saying stuff like "oh well look at them they have a degree".
I am trying my best.
So please give me a rest.
Because I'm doing the best I can.
I've been trying since the day my mental health began.
But I can't please everyone and that's okay.
That's something I've had to learn the hard way.

No place like home

I never really understood the old saying "there's no place like home"
Until I was taken away from all I've ever known.
Struggling with mental health is a challenge every single day.
But this new challenge hurts in a different way.
I am hours away from home detained under the mental health act.
Meaning I can't leave and that's a fact.
Some days are harder than others, but I miss my home every day.
And home doesn't have to be a building or place,
it can be a person you want to stay.
Being in an unknown environment can bring up
so many negative emotions such as fear.
Fear that you are somewhere far away and
your home is nowhere near.
It can be so daunting and scary being sent hours away.
When all you want to do is stay.
So the saying there's no place like home can be many things.
Being sent far, far away really does sting.
All I want is to be at home with my family where I belong.
Because my stay here could be very, very long.
And I will work day and night to fight to get out of here.
So that I can go home and I can reappear.
To the ones I love and the ones who love me.
When I finally leave here I will truly be set free.

Breakdown to Breakthrough

I have gone from a breakdown to a breakthrough.
Even when I couldn't see a way through.
Yes, I still suffer massively with my mental health.
And there are still days I don't feel myself.
But just as the title of this book,
I do have a story of strength, so let's take a look.
I turned my pain into poetry.
To help the world see what I see.
The idea of my first book was to do three important things.
Maybe even convince people to not gain their wings.
One, I want some of the mental health stigma to be broken.
Because I want to advocate and I refuse to remain unspoken.
To raise some awareness to a topic that is highly misunderstood.
So maybe there can be more bad than good.
And last but not least number three.
I want to give people hope and be set free.
My book won't change the world, but I hope it
can help even just one person out there.
For them to know that there is light at the end
of a tunnel and people do care.
I still have days where I struggle.
I still have negative emotions I'm trying to juggle.
But publishing my first book was my biggest success.
I published a book while sectioned and everything was a mess.
So in many ways I believe I went
from a breakdown to a breakthrough.
Because this book was the making of me and
it made me see a way through.
Despite what you're going through or what anyone says.
You can achieve anything and you can see success.
If I can publish a book while sectioned in
the hospital you can do anything.
So go ahead and chase your dreams and
believe me it's worth everything.

So to answer my own question, did I go
from a breakdown to breakthrough?
To be honest I'm not sure but in many ways I think I do.
Being in and out of the emergency department and acute wards.
Self-harming, attempting my life and
not living a life with any awards.
But publishing my first book pain into poetry
May not be considered a breakdown to breakthrough,
but it really did set me free.
Because for once in my life I felt proud.
And I actually looked at my achievement and I was wowed.
Despite everything I still managed to achieve something huge.
And I'm not miserable everyday like Scrooge.
Breakdown to Breakthroughs, believe me it can happen.
You can see the beautiful colours when everything blackened.

The system

The mental health system is absolutely broken.
And I refuse to remain unspoken.
Even when I've been on death's door in the ICU.
They still refuse to help you.
I lay on what could have been my death bed.
Yet they would still rather send me home with no support instead.
I remember them coming to see me in intensive care.
And I said with so much effort "help me"
And they did nothing, and it's not fair.
So many people go into ICU and don't make it out alive.
Because there was too much damage done
to their body for them to survive.
People try to take their lives every single day.
Yet the system still turns them away.
I understand the NHS is stretched to the absolute limits.
But people are attempting their life every single minute.
Every 31 seconds Google says someone attempts suicide.
Every 31 seconds someone tries to take their life.
Because they couldn't see the light.
Yet the system still won't help them fight.
I know they're stretched, understaffed and probably underpaid.
But they still refuse to help even when we pick up that blade.
And when we are afraid.
Of what we might do because of the thoughts in our head.
They can take over and easily spread.
And make you do something that you might regret.
And it can cause so much trauma and upset.
But I don't want this poem to feel like I am blaming
those who work in mental health.
Many of them are angels and life savers for when you're not yourself.
It's just sad to see how stretched they are.
And they don't have the resources to help those,
the system isn't perfect, very, very far from it.

It's just so sad to see.
And you may even disagree.
But the mental health system needs to change.
Because people's lives are at stake.

Turn something bad into something beautiful

I have faced so much bad in my life.
And it makes me so sad and so mad.
It feels like I'm being stabbed in the back with a knife.
You see when you throw a rock in the ocean
you don't know how far it goes.
And it's the exact same for words, your words could
hurt someone and you'd never even know.
Suffering with mental health comes with its bad days.
And this isn't some attention-seeking act or a phrase.
I have faced so much stigma and judgement from society.
And even sometimes by those who claim "they love me".
You see, this world can be a very judgmental place.
And when I am judged it really puts a frown on my face.
For so long I didn't know how to cope with
not only the stigma but how I feel.
Because to you it might be nothing, but to me it is real.
I have developed so many bad coping
mechanisms that do more harm than good.
All I want is to be treated equally and be understood.
But not too long ago I found a love for poetry.
So I can help people see what I see.
And then I decided why not publish a book.
So that way people can read and take a look.
I have three goals when it comes to my book.
1. Break some stigma
2. Raise some awareness
3. Give hope
You see there is a lot of stigma attached to mental health.
It should be normalised to say "I don't feel myself".
One in four of us will suffer from a mental health condition at some
point in our life, so if it's not you it could be someone you care about.
So raising some awareness can help millions no doubt.

But I also want to give hope.
To people who feel they can no longer cope.
And to remind them that they are never truly alone.
They could be hurting just like that stone.
I would like to think I've turned my experience with
mental illness into something beautiful.
And maybe even meaningful.
You see bad can be turned into good.
And I think we should all stick together and remain standing.

Why

You may ask what inspired me to write a book.
So why don't we take a deeper look.
I write poetry in the hope that others will see what I see.
My goal of this book was to do one of three things.
Number one gets some of the stigma around mental health broken.
Because I want to advocate for us and I refuse to remain unspoken.
Number two to raise some awareness about mental health.
And how anyone can struggle, no matter your
age, gender, background or even wealth.
And that it should be normalised to not feel ourselves.
And last but not least to give hope to those
touched by mental illness.
So that in times when they can't cope they can be
reminded that they are never truly alone.
A lot of my poems are raw and real.
Hard hitting because this is how I feel.
While some may consider them depressing and sad.
I write them to remind others that they're
not alone and things aren't all bad.
As hard as it may be to relate.
It reminds people they are not the only one in that mental state.
On the other hand, a lot of my poems aim for positivity.
Because through my book I have a duty.
To encourage people to keep going and to stick around.
And to remind them that their happiness can be found.
And it may take time and be a hard battle to fight.
But I want to remind people there is light.
I had been writing poetry long before I decided to begin
the process of publishing a book for the world to see.
I didn't know where to start, I was scared of rejection but I figured
if I don't try I won't know and everyone around me agreed.
I got a lot of encouragement from staff and patients
at the hospital, my family and friends.

People I've come into contact with at the
hardest of times, the list never ends.
So in the end I decided to bite the bullet.
And just do it.
I contacted the head of the UK publishers to share my
poetry and how I want to share it with the world.
And they agreed to take a look and even then I already felt proud.
I sent them over my book, from start to finish.
They got back to me saying this was something they could publish.
They went through and read every single word.
Edited it to make sure it was perfect and it could be heard.
They asked me questions such as, what audience is the book for,
an overview of what the book is about and more.
I sent them the "blurb" which goes on the back and gives a
short but strong overview of what the book is about.
They also designed many front covers and
I chose the one that stood out.
It is a picture of me smiling, and I want that to show
that in the darkest of times you can still smile.
Even if you're suffering with your mental
health and negative emotions pile.
And this is currently where I stand.
It didn't feel real until I saw the front and back cover, but
I live for the day I can hold that book in my hand.
I couldn't have done this without the help of so many
people who encouraged me to chase my dream.
They believed in me when they didn't and made us feel like a team.
I don't see this achievement as just mine.
Because if it wasn't for the help and encouragement
of others I wouldn't even have a front design.
My experience at Cygnet has been beyond words.
Staff have always printed my poems off no matter how
many times I asked even if it got on their nerves.

Not only that but they saw and still see all the good in me.
They see my talents and flaws even when I was too blinded to see.
They have always noticed when I wasn't okay.
And they are always available for a chat no matter night or day.
And my favourite thing about being on the ward.
There are so many groups so we are never bored.
Even when I don't have the energy to go and I force myself.
I always feel better afterwards and it improves my mental health.
If I have one thing to say, it is if you believe you can
achieve, which is one of my poems.
And I'm glad I took my own advice in the end.
Because if I can publish a book while
sectioned three hours away from home,
You can do anything, the possibilities never end.
So go and do your dream and make yourself proud.
Because when you achieve, you might be surprised, but also wowed,
And always remember, there's only one of you standing in a crowd.

Teenage troubles

I like to preach about the importance of mental health.
And how it is so important we speak.
And how anyone can be affected no matter age,
gender or even wealth.
And by expressing how we feel does not make us weak.
Now this poem is dedicated to age.
And no matter how old you are.
You can still feel emotions like sadness, anxiety, loneliness and rage.
And maybe you feel suicidal and have
thoughts about being hit by a car.
A group that I believe is at high risk of
mental health is those in their teens.
Because they are put under so much pressure to get good grades.
And they spend so much time on their phones and screens.
While a lot of them might be thinking about picking up that blade.
While it's okay to be on screens as social media is a way we connect.
It can also be toxic as a lot of cyberbullying can take place.
And it can have a real negative effect.
And what once was your safe space has now been replaced.
Bullying alone is most common in the teenage years.
And it is what I believe to be one of the lead
causes of deaths in teens today.
Because of all the sleepless nights and tears.
Of reading hate comments online or being
scared to go to school the next day.
School alone I believe can be a contribution to bad mental health
As teachers put students under so much pressure,
Making them go home and then they don't feel their self.
Because they have so much homework from their professor.
And it can feel as if they never ever get a break.
You go to school and go home and you're meant to relax.
But with all the homework and assignments
it puts your mental health at stake.
It can lead to a lot of anxiety, even panic attacks.

And there's this expectation to be in the popular group in school.
And not be classed as the weird and nerdy kids
who sit at the back of the class.
Because you wanna be known as funny and cool.
Not just the nerds whose only goal is to pass.
But these groups are detrimental to our mental
health, we should all come together as one.
Because the pressure to fit into certain
groups can cause so much stress.
I don't believe there is a need for groups, no need for none.
Because it can cause so much stress, tension and aggression.
Teachers put too much pressure on you, making you
think these exams determine the rest of your life.
When that is actually far from the truth and they actually
need to recognise you're trying your best and be nice.
School, exams, grades, pressure, relationships,
are not worth your mental health.
And categorising people into groups is not important,
such as who has the best wealth.
But not only that, it's time to recognise teenagers
can suffer with mental health conditions too.
It shouldn't be turned away or put down to hormones
or puberty simply because of their age.
Or the fact they're under stress and have loads of homework due.
They could be suffering with a serious
illness that could be at any stage.
Teenagers' mental health matters too, and it's time
we recognise the stress they are put under.
To achieve good grades, go to college, uni,
get a job and earn good money.
To fit in with their peers, balance all this
life and then we sit and really wonder
Why they are suffering, because the expectation of them
is too much, in school it's not all about being funny.

We need to put teens under less and less stress because
when it comes to their mental health it can be fatal.
The leading cause of death for young people aged
between ten and nineteen is suicide.
When what we really need is support available so
we can ensure teens' mental health is stable.
And we are not losing more and more lives to suicide because it was
simply brushed off as hormones, we really need
to be looking at the other side.
And we can't say stuff like, "oh they just want attention" because
that's what I was told when I was sixteen by a CAMHS professional.
I was told I was too young to be suffering with
any form of mental illness.
And that alone caused my mental health to
be worse and detrimental.
Because I wouldn't have been told those
things if it was a physical illness.
Four years on I am now 20 and I still suffer massively.
And I look back at how I was treated and it was not okay.
And I don't want any youth to go through what I did being
told it's in their head and they have no capacity.
Teenagers matter too, and we need to let them
speak and have their say.
I truly feel sorry for my younger self.
While everyone believed I was faking,
I was actually suffering with my mental health.
So this stigma around teenagers' mental health is
something I really think is worth breaking.
Hence why I wrote this poem, and I will continue to write more.
Because I will advocate for us all.
Because we deserve better.
Mental health in youths isn't something we should ignore.
Because without help and treatment they can become suicidal,
and might even consider writing their suicide letter.
Like I once did when I was sixteen.

Because no one believed me.
So my only option was to leave.
I just wanted to be set free.
So let's be the change the system needs.
So teens don't turn to stuff like self-harm.
And they don't end up cutting themselves until it bleeds.
And have forever scars on their arms.
Having to explain to their kids.
As to why there are white lines.
As if suffering with mental health as a teen is forbidden.
It's about time we make a change and start to recognise the signs.

Urge surfing

You know when you have urges to self-harm
And you so desperately want to cut your arm.
And you can't seem to get rid of that urge.
And you feel it's taking over you and can't emerge.
But one way I like to view these urges is that it's just like a wave.
And one fighting that urge is so brave.
You see, waves they can get big and really, really high.
And surfers will go on that wave and they
may feel like they're going to die.
Kind of how if I don't give into these self-harm urges, I feel I may
die and it makes me want to cry and I can't even explain why.
But when surfers decide to take that ride.
It's so hard but even if they don't manage
to ride the wave, at least they tried.
Same goes for self-harm, if you don't manage to fight the
urge don't beat yourself up because at least you tried.
One thing I want you to picture is a wave and how when it
gets so big it eventually calms and you won't drown.
And the same goes for urges, they may be so strong
in the present but they will calm down.
I'm not saying these urges aren't real because I've had them myself.
And it can take a massive toll on your mental health.
But the point I'm trying to make is that these urges won't last.
And there will come a time when they were simply in the past.
At the moment it can feel so hard to fight.
Because you can get these urges day or night.
But if I want you to take one thing away from
this is that these urges won't last forever.
Just like waves don't last forever.
Hence why we call urge surfing, we feel the urge that is so real.
And really plays a part into how we feel.
But we ride out the urge until it goes.
And before you know it, you ride the wave, you fought
the urge and now you can put this to a close.

And you may have to do this multiple times a day.
But that is completely okay.
Because believe me there is a way.
Through urge surfing we identify that intense
feeling of self-harm will go away.

Equality

You see when people think of the word equality
they think of treating everyone the same.
But that's not actually what it is, it means treating everyone
with equal respect and care without any shame.
Equality isn't something I've experienced, I've experienced
inequality in many places and many times.
All because of my mental health, they treat me like
suffering with mental illness is a crime.
All I long for is to be treated like anyone else
and not be discriminated against.
Because I have been discriminated against in many
settings when all I'm doing is trying my best.
In school, in college, they made me feel people
like me don't deserve a place in society.
They caused me so much upset, hatred of self and anxiety.
They made me feel like I'm never going to be
worthy of getting a degree or having a job.
Because all they see when they look at me is mental
illness and the girl who always sobs.
Emergency departments are for anyone in need of an emergency.
Same goes for an ambulance.
But when it's a mental health emergency
They treat you so horribly.
And that makes me feel scared to ask for support.
That's where I turn to as a last resort.
When using my skills or taking my pills haven't worked.
Or calling a helpline or talking to a friend.
None of it worked in the end.
With how I've been treated it makes me
wanna curl up into a ball and die.
Because when I think about the mistreatment
I've faced I just wanna cry.
I suffer with mental health, that doesn't
make me a criminal or a bad person.

And when you treat me like one it just
makes my mental health worsen.
I am sweet, kind, polite and caring.
But to you when you hear the word "mental health"
you think we are aggressive and rude.
And it really does lower my mood.
I am not mean and I wouldn't hurt a fly.
The only one I hurt is myself and you question why
When I get treated so horribly and so badly.
But this is the state of the NHS sadly.
A&E doctors, nurses, GPs, paramedics and police.
All need a basic understanding of mental health I believe.
The amount of times I have to go to the emergency departments
alone begging for help and I get treated so bad.
It genuinely breaks my heart and makes me so sad and mad.
Yet when I do advocate for myself and my mental health.
The second I pipe up I am seen as rude and
get security called on myself.
When all I am doing is saying this is now how we should be treated.
I am not aggressive when I speak and this just
makes me feel deafened and weak.
Because no matter what I do or what I say.
You'll always find a way to discriminate anyway.
It makes me scared to ask for help and
support and that is so wrong.
When all I want is to be treated equally with kindness all along.
When they hear the word "mental health patient"
I feel they get this idea in their head.
That we are going to be a challenge but
we are often the opposite instead.
Personally for me when I've attended the emergency department
for mental health I have always been polite and nice.
But I don't get the same back, and I get the complete
opposite and it's not even been once or twice.
It's been so many times I've lost count at this point.

We fall to the hands of the mental health system and they disappoint.
Even when I've been on death's door in the ICU.
The system still refuses to help you.
I can think of so many times I've been treated horribly.
Surely this isn't allowed and it's not morally correct.
And it really does have a negative effect.
We come to get help and we are meant to leave
feeling better, that's the whole hospital point.
While with physical health that's the case, when it
comes to mental health they disappoint.
But believe me mental health emergencies are
extremely common in today's society.
And the group's mental health impacts are a wide variety.
Even community mental health teams can treat you badly.
But it's the truth of the system sadly.
Something has to change because lives are
being lost and lives are at stake.
But you still refuse to help no matter our mental state.
Sometimes it feels like I have to do something
drastic to get the help I need.
But even when I was in a coma for five days once I was "medically
cleared" I was sent away with nothing, no support at all agreed.
I find myself in a vicious cycle of asking for help,
being treated badly, feeling worse.
And I just go round and round and it's like an evil curse.
I have so much anger towards the system and believe me I
understand they're understaffed, overworked and underpaid.
But that's not our fault and we still shouldn't feel afraid.
But truth be told, I'm scared, very, very scared.
Because I don't believe a lot of people
who work in these places ever cared.
Now please don't take this the wrong way.
Because there are good people out there who truly care every day.
But in times of crisis and alone we fall to
the hands of the mental health system.

And one of the things they fail to do most is listen.
They fail to keep us safe when we are clearly a danger to ourselves.
And we are very clearly suffering with our mental health.
But they would rather label it off as dramatic.
These experiences I've had are so traumatic.
And I think about them every day when I go to sleep.
And all I can do is lay there and weep.
Because yes I have had good experiences, but
believe me I've had more bad than good.
And as much as I try to focus on the good, I still feel misunderstood.
I am a person, with a heart, and kind one is what you'll find.
But because I am a "mental health patient"
you think I'm going to be unkind.
But you don't even give me a chance to show my true self.
While I may struggle with my mental health,
that doesn't make me bad.
And the fact people think that really does make me sad.
It brings tears to my eyes and makes me want to cry.
And I don't even know why because
most of these people are strangers.
So why should I care what they think?
Why should I care when they send me to a shrink.
But I do, I do care because I'm painted out to be someone I'm not.
And with how the system treats us it just
makes me wanna hide in my bed and rot.

My mum

Being away from my mum breaks my heart.
To know that we could be together right now but we are apart.
No matter how old I get I will always need my mum.
Without her I feel so empty and numb.
I will work day and night to fight to get out of here.
Not just for me but so I can reunite with my mum and be near.
I love you, Mum, and I will do everything in
my power for us to be together again.
And until that day comes just know I love you,
I wish I could know when.
Know when we can finally reunite, not for a
couple of hours or days but for good.
Because when I am around you I feel truly understood.

My own advice

For so long I wrote poems giving motivation and advice.
But it took me ages for me to look twice.
I wrote a poem called "if you believe and you can achieve"
And it's ironic really because I never did believe it.
I was happily giving hope and motivation to everyone but myself.
Preaching about how important it is to talk about our mental health.
In the end I took my own advice and
decided to try and publish a book.
So I can share my poetry with the world and they can take a look.
I want to break stigma, raise awareness and give hope
For those touched by my mental illness when they can't cope.
But to also show others that mental health is real.
And we all have emotions we need to feel.
I was scared of rejection and people
thinking they weren't anyone good.
But then I remember J.K. Rowling was denied
many times but in the end she stood.
She stood tall because she is one of the best authors out there.
So go ahead and do what you want to do because
you might think it's rare.
But it is possible.

mental illness

It is a disease of the mind
And it is not kind is what you'll find.
Mental illness can take lives due to suicide.
Because their illness looked over them and they died.
Some say suicide is an act of selfishness as
we are leaving people behind.
When we die others will suffer but you have to
understand we have had a disease of the mind.
Now you wouldn't be mad if we chose to
end our life due to a physical disease.
But mental health is seen differently, even if
we are begging for help on our knees.
I don't believe anyone who commits
suicide actually wanted to actually die.
What they wanted was their pain to be gone, and they didn't
see that happening, so their only option was to fly high.
When it comes to mental illness the grief people
experience from it can be turned into blame.
Or they may even feel ashamed to say their loved ones died that way.
The brain is a vital organ, just like the lungs and the heart.
And when it fails, everything can fall apart
Often leading to extreme suffering and even death.
And in the end it can lead to someone taking their very last breath.
I think when people are in pain and desperate for the pain to end.
And they can no longer put on a brave face and pretend.
They take action, I don't think they often
think about what they're about to do.
Not realising it can lead to death and they didn't intend to leave you.

Never in a million years

Never in a million years.
All those sleepless nights full of tears.
Never in a million years I can't stop saying that phrase.
Because I truly never believed I would ever get praise.
But people are telling me they are proud.
And honestly truth be told I am wowed.
You see when you suffer with mental health our
brains convince us we can't achieve.
But that is just a cruel lie from the brain and often
society, all you have to do is believe.
As I said before, never in a million years did I think this was possible.
But I did in-fact do the impossible.
And as much as I don't wanna say it, I am proud of myself.
Because I achieved something massive despite my mental health.
The sense of achievement is wonderful but you
know what's even more impressive.
When you achieve something through difficult
circumstances, for me I am very depressive.
But I never let that stop me or get in my way
Because I live to see the day.
That I achieve my dream and it becomes my reality.
I did this even if I felt I was losing my sanity.
So yes, never in a million years did I think I could
do this, but you won't know if you don't try.
So instead of wasting time asking why me and you start to cry.
Why not have a goal or a dream you want to fulfil.
Instead of waiting there while you stand still.
Because the clock will keep ticking and the world will go by.
So why not give it a go and try.
I have shocked myself with what I can do.
Even when I didn't see a way through.
And you might be asking "what is it that you did that was so great",
What was it that put you in this positive mental state?
So why don't I tell you and we can take a deeper look.

What I did was publish a book.
And while that's not that big of a deal.
I can't put into words how it made me feel.
I didn't just publish a book but I did this publishing
process while being sectioned far far away.
And there were many times I questioned
if I'd make it through the day.
And my book consists of mental health
poetry just like this poem right here.
To show people that they are not alone, from one
suffering person to another, I am near.
I did a lot of my poetry writing while
I was in the community and at home.
But I also did a lot of it while in hospital as it
helped me get through the day alone.
It also sort of tells a story of my life as I often write about how
I was feeling/what was going on in my life at that point.
And I really wanted to achieve something not just for
me but for my family as I don't want to disappoint.
So this is what I was talking about
when I said never in a million years.
Just because we have a mental health condition
doesn't mean we can't have careers.
I have to admit my idea of success looks very
different from what I thought years ago.
But publishing this book makes me feel proud when I feel low.
It's a reminder to never ever give up hope.
And I will always remember these achievements
when I feel I can't cope.

Dream to reality

For so long this was just a dream.
I never believed it would come true.
But having this dream happen has allowed
me to see life from a different view.
If I've learned anything it is that we all need a purpose.
And the idea of that may make you feel nervous.
But having a goal, having something to work for.
Gives you a reason to wake up in the morning
and it just gives you a feeling you can't ignore.
As someone who suffers with their mental health
and often felt there was no point in going on.
Having a purpose I found to be so beneficial
and really showed me I do belong.
I believe we all have something to offer
this world whether we see it or not.
And I will keep reminding you in case you forgot.
One thing I struggle with is suicidal thoughts and tendencies.
It's like living and existing is my worst enemy.
It's a heartbreaking feeling to wake up and not want to be alive.
And it feels like you are just trying to survive.
And we don't get enough credit for simply choosing to stay.
We find it so hard to just get through to the end of the day.
Having a dream won't fix everything but it will give me a reason.
A reason to wake up and live my life no matter the season.
It's so heartwarming when your dream turns into reality.
You can do anything if you have the right mentality.
I never believed this was something I could do.
I never believed this dream would come true.
It was just a distant dream for so long.
But I ended up proving myself so wrong.
This has really boosted my self-worth.
And it gives me a reason to stay on this earth.
So I will keep writing.
And I will keep fighting.

Every word, every verse.
I want to be heard so things don't get worse.
I'm glad in the end I decided to just do it.
Because I surprised myself, I have to admit.
I felt like a kid when I went to the store.
It felt like a dream come true as soon as I walked through the door.
This time it's a little different as I'm older.
I have to carry a lot of weight on my shoulder.
But I did do it and sometimes I am in disbelief.
But at the same time I feel a lot of relief.
Because after months and months of me dreaming this dream.
It happened, and in the end I saw the light and it gleamed.

Mental health

Mental health, we all have it.
And it's hard, I must admit.
It's kind of like how we all have physical health.
It's okay if you don't quite feel yourself.
There is so much stigma and prejudice around this topic.
It's okay if we are anxious, depressed or even psychotic.
So anxious that we feel our heart is about to pound out our chest.
While you might stand there not impressed, we are trying our best.
We may feel so depressed we can't leave our bed.
And we have certain thoughts in our head.
Maybe we are experiencing psychosis which
means we are becoming more ill.
But we just want to be treated like everyone else,
we can still have goals we want to fulfil.
From some low mood to feeling like life isn't worth living.
We all deserve support from the very beginning.
Mental health doesn't define who we are.
And I know our recovery can seem so far.
But believe me it can and will.
Our life doesn't have to be all about being ill.
Sometimes my mental health diagnosis feels like a prison sentence.
and I am determined to get back my independence.
There is more to life than my mental health condition.
And I will keep fighting no matter my position.
Because I want my life back, I want to be happy.
Not depressed and snappy.
And I work day and night.
And I will never give up my fight.

The ending won't change

I walk myself to the pub late at night.
And I'm asking myself if this is right.
Will the drink help me fight?
Maybe not, or maybe it just might.
Will I find the answers I want at the bottom of a drink?
Or will I just end up puking in the sink.
So drunk I can't even think.
Or maybe I need to see a shrink.
I go to the pub every night, have the same drink and the same shots.
And I don't just have one or two, I have lots and lots.
And I don't know when to stop.
And I think to myself this night will be different but it never changes.
I just end up getting drunk and telling my life story to strangers.
Everyone around me says you know it will always end the same.
And I'm the only one I can blame.
But really what is my aim?
Because right now I feel nothing but shame.
One thing I always get told is that alcohol is a depressant.
And it affects your medication when you take antidepressants.
But in the moment when I'm doing shot after shot.
My mind starts to go away and I actually forgot.
I forgot about all my problems because it's the moment I live for.
But I know eventually I'll end up passed out on the floor.
But at the moment I feel on top of the world.
And my brain feels a bit twirled.
And the more I have, the more I crave.
And I start to feel so confident and brave.
Like nothing can hurt me, I am invincible.
But then later on I feel worse than I did and I am miserable.
At the moment I feel so happy that nothing can bring me down.
I got a great big smile on my face instead of a frown.
But I need to remind myself one thing.
Is that later on this will really sting.
Because I'll feel worse than I did before.

I can't just drink my emotions away and ignore.
It's better to fight instead.
Not just drown them out of my head.
I know the ending will never change and I'll always feel worse.
And I'll end up in A&E because I've done
something stupid and I need a nurse.
When I drink I become impulsive and I do things I regret.
but I always end up saying I forget.
And I do, alcohol affects your memory.
I need to make alcohol not my best friend, but my enemy.

What I miss

I miss my old life, life with my family at home.
Because being at home is all I've ever known.
I miss my life outside of the hospital.
I wish I could be on holiday somewhere tropical.
But I can't leave the country because I'm detained.
In a place where you can be injected and physically restrained.
Hours away from my hometown.
Where I had family and friends all around.
I miss my freedom to do what I like.
But you can't just do what you want when you're psych.
You get told when to sleep, when to eat.
A place where it's so hard to get back on your feet.
I miss my family every single minute of every single day.
When they come to visit I wish they
didn't have to leave and they could stay.
I miss them all the time and it makes me cry.
But I really am going to try.
To get back to the family where I belong.
And all I can do until then is stay strong.
Every day feels like a week, every week feels like an hour.
I feel so helpless in my situation, like I have no power.
There is so much more to life than these four walls.
Walking up and down the same goddamn halls.
I miss my hometown, although I used to call it a shit hole.
Being away from where I grew up and where I've
lived for 20 years and it's all out of my control.
I miss my bed and not having to sleep on what
I would describe as a PE mat in school.
I miss being in college and having a purpose,
now I feel like a useless tool.
I miss going out with friends, shopping and going for food.
Now I feel so isolated and it just lowers my mood.
I'm in a place where you can be stopped from going outside.
A place where you lose all of freedom, dignity and pride.

A place where staff make mean and
heartless comments without any care.
A place where you watch people lose their lives
to the system and it is not far.
A place where you can be forced to take medication against your will.
A place where you are sectioned just
because someone says you are ill.
A place that feels more like a prison.
I don't know how I'll ever get through this admission.
Because sometimes it feels as if it is pure torture.
A place where you are under a section order.
I miss my old life so much because there is no life here.
A place where you are in constant suffering and fear.
When I should be out there with my family and be near.
I should be out in the real world getting a career.
I will fight day in and day out to get out of this place.
The day I walk out those doors I will
have a great big smile on my face.

Why are you mad?

One thing I can't understand.
Is why I self-harm you get mad.
Because that actually makes me really sad.
You see, I am trying my best.
Please just give me a rest.
This isn't supposed to be some kind of test.
A test to see what I decide to do.
When I am feeling so blue.
Instead of being mad you should ask yourself why.
Why did this patient decide to harm themselves and cry?
Instead of shouting at us and saying you're angry or disappointed.
Maybe just tell them it's okay and think
how this could have been avoided.
Sit with us, be with us instead of shout.
Because that is not what care and treatment is all about.

Star

Star, you are exactly what your name is, a star.
And I know in life you would have gone so far.
I remember we all used to call you star bar.
I would do anything to change the fact you were in that car.
I know towards the end I didn't see you very much.
As we both got older I guess we just lost touch.
But that doesn't mean I never thought about you.
Your death feels so hard to accept, I wish it wasn't true.
I think part of me was in denial that you could be taken so soon.
I will never forget that afternoon.
But when I saw your name scattered all over the news.
That's when it became real.
And I can't even put into words how I feel.
I am still in so much shock days later.
The hole in my heart could not get any greater.
When I heard that someone close to me had died
you were the last person I would have thought.
I just feel so broken and distraught.
You were seventeen, you had so much life ahead of you.
You had dreams and goals to pursue.
We spent so much time together growing up.
It felt like you were my sister and not my niece.
I felt roles were reversed and you took care of me,
and now you will rest in peace.
Now you're gone I think of all the things I wish I could have done.
I wish I could have been a better aunt, I wish it was
just a bad dream that could be undone.
You were taken at such a young age.
I feel so many emotions, sadness, anger, devastation and rage.
Why did it have to be you, they wrote on
the news you had a heart of gold.
And that couldn't have been worded better,
that's the truth to be told.

It breaks my heart you had to be taken
in such a tragic and devastating way.
You were one month away from your 18th birthday in May.
I can't stop asking myself if you were in pain,
did you know you were going to die.
But I know asking myself these questions
will just make me suffer and cry.
I'm sorry that the last time you saw me was
when I was in hospital.
I'm sorry that's the last memory you have of me.
If I knew that was the last time I'd see you I would have
hugged tighter, I wish this wasn't the way it had to be.
My favourite memory of us is us skipping the queue at Thorpe Park.
We had no patience, I remember when
we went on the rides in the dark.
You loved all the twists and turns and had no fear.
It was actually you who got me over my fear of
rides but I felt safe because you were near.
I loved being your aunt and no matter how many years
go by you'll always hold a special place in my heart.
I'm sorry you were taken so soon, it devastates me we are apart.
I love you, Star, and I will miss you every
single day till the day I die.
Because we are family, we share the same last name,
every time I look up and see a star in the sky.
I will think of you, because I do and always will love you.

Life beyond the ward

I think about the day I am discharged and I leave the ward.
It will feel absolutely freeing, it will be a massive, massive award.
There is a big, big world waiting for me to return.
And maybe there are still things for me to learn.
But I want to go back into the world, whether I feel ready or not.
Because honestly being here is a lot.
I've seen things, I've heard things that to be
honest have absolutely destroyed me.
And not just destroy me but traumatise me, I want to be free.
And these things you can't help them from
happening nor can you prevent.
And sometimes I feel I need a place where I can vent.
But I can't, because the things I want to vent about are
the hospital, and the system which is so broken.
And I am the sort of person if I see something wrong
I won't remain unspoken.
No one can change what's happened, I want to move forward.
I need to keep going, onward and upward.
There is so much life waiting for me, and this
book is the start of many achievements.
Because that's what I miss most, the sense of achievement.
When I did well in school and college I felt so proud.
And because I always put myself down I was truly wowed.
And while being an author isn't being in
education or having a degree.
It has still given me my purpose back you see.
I loved school and college when it came to doing so well.
But then things changed when I started to become unwell.
It was hard to focus on the future when I was
only trying to get through the day.
Me questioning my life and if I should go or stay.
When you struggle with suicidal ideation it
is near impossible to look ahead.
Because you have got a war going on in your head.

Making you question your existence on this earth.
Making you seriously question your worth.
I have also faced a lot of mental health stigma from people.
They treat me like I am a horrible person or even a criminal.
They make me feel like my mental health
diagnosis is a prison sentence.
But we are just as capable and have our independence.
During education they weren't very understanding and they
made me feel like someone like me doesn't belong in society.
They treated me so unfairly to everyone
else causing me so much anxiety.
With how I was discriminated against and how I was treated.
It made me not want to do anything else, I felt so defeated.
It sent me into depression, I never believed
I would ever do anything good.
I never believed anyone would understand.
I didn't get out of bed so much that my mattress had a
dip down the middle where I constantly laid there.
I didn't eat, or drink, and when I did it was always
takeaways, I never went out, I didn't care.
I didn't wash, or change my clothes,
I had lost all care for myself.
I took attempts on my life due to declining mental health.
one which was fatal and what I consider to be near death.
I really believed I'd take my last breath.
I was constantly in and out of A&E and mental crises,
it felt like a vicious cycle I couldn't break.
And then my biggest fear of being in wards and sectioning
came true, I wish it was just a dream and I could wake up.
I've been in for months, I know it's like being stripped of
everyone, your belongings, your freedom to go outside.
Looking at all my stuff, dignity and pride.
Get told what meds to take, when to eat and sleep.

When I want is to go back into the world but I
can't, so I just sit in my room and weep.
I live for the day I can back out into the real
world because this is not it.
And it's not even close I must admit.
I'm sick and tired of the same goddamn walls.
Pacing up and down the same looking halls.
I cannot wait for the day I am discharged and I can
be free and live my life to the best I can.
Because my story is far from over, it's only just begun.

It's not weak to speak

If there is one thing I want to preach.
It is that there is nothing more powerful than your speech.
When it comes to mental health the best thing you can do is speak.
And believe me when I say it is not bad or weak.
Mental health isn't something that should have to stay hidden.
As if suffering with a mental illness is wrong or forbidden.
There is a stigma that talking about how
we feel is a sign of us being weak.
But that is far from the truth when some support
and understanding is all we seek.
Personally I think speaking about our
mental health is brave and strong.
But in today's society people act like it is bad and wrong.
But don't listen to the stigma and speak about how you feel.
Because I know for me and you it feels real.
I'm just one person and speak for thousands
when it comes to mental health.
And I want people to know it's okay if they don't feel their self.
Speaking out in my opinion is the bravest thing you can do.
Because you're never alone and there is a way through.
So as I said before it is not weak to speak.
You are valued on this earth even if you don't see your worth.
So don't hide away and don't hide your suffering and pain.
Because your feelings matter, you can speak about
whatever is going on inside your brain.

Justice

I have been in the mental health system for many years.
So many sleepless nights full of tears.
From A&E, to crisis team, to community mental health teams.
To mental health hospitals where there
are constant alarms and screams.
There have been countless times I have felt neglected and failed.
Sometimes this doesn't even feel like a hospital.
It feels like I've been jailed.
So many restrictions on what you can do.
Sometimes I struggle to see a way through.
I ask myself how they even got this job in the first place.
Because so many of them are just a disgrace.
This is not care, this is neglect and abuse.
And they will go looking for any excuse.
Any excuse of how the blame can be put
on us and it's us who is at fault.
Because they don't want to admit their staff are
in the wrong, this is worse than assault.
So many heartless and mean comments have been made.
Yet they get rewarded for this job because at the end
of the month it's them who gets paid.
Paid to do what exactly, neglect their patients and
make jokes that should never have been said.
When they should be helping us and encouraging us instead.
You think it can't get any worse but then
something happens that shocks me.
This isn't fair because all I want is to be set free.
I have seen it all, and heard it all at this point.
And the mental health system does disappoint.
They will happily talk about my mistakes and what I've done wrong.
But they refuse to admit the mistakes of their staff all along.
When I break the rules, I'm the bad guy.
But when they break the rules they brush
it under the carpet and go shy.

Because these people wouldn't dream of admitting their mistake.
Because at the end of the day it's their job at stake.
They will always find a reason to blame me instead.
Telling me this is all not true and it's all in my head.
They will be angry and judge you for things like self-harm.
Like when you need help and you press the alarm.
But instead of being angry and cross they
should be understanding and kind.
And ask themselves why they do this, they may have
certain thoughts and feelings in their mind.
Justice must be served because this is far from okay.
And I will keep screaming what they've done until I see the day.
The day where they are held accountable for their actions.
And I want to see all of their reactions.
Because they act like they are untouchable
and cannot be held accountable.
But this type of behaviour cannot be allowable.
I will scream and shout about my experience in the system.
Because at the end of the day I am the victim.
I will tell the whole world what goes on behind closed doors.
And I will never stop talking about my experience with these words.
I may never get justice but I will for sure not stay silent.
Because I am a patient, yet I get treated like a criminal and violent.
I will advocate and I will tell the truth about my experience.
And I will not let this go because this is a topic that is very serious.

The domino effect

The domino effect is something that happens on the psych ward.
It can start as someone simply being bored and feeling ignored.
Just like a row of dominoes when one falls
it knocks the other ones down.
And that is what happens on the ward all around.
When one person starts to struggle it can trigger the rest.
Because we are all here for our own reasons and trying our best.
We don't ever like to say the Q word which is quiet.
Suddenly everything can be okay and then it becomes like a riot.
People can easily be triggered by what
others do which creates the domino effect.
A lot goes on in these wards, a lot of abuse and neglect.
Every day is different on the ward, no two days are the same.
But we all have the same goal and same aim.
And that is to one day leave here, and live a life free of this ward.
Because we want our true self to show and be restored.
You even know what you're going to wake up to here.
Staff never know what they're walking into doing this type of career.
The domino effect is something we all fear and we all dread.
We would much rather the ward be calm and quiet instead.
It's something that can't be helped and
it's those days that are so hard.
It's those days that make us wish we could leave this place,
and it's those days that leave the best of us scarred.

The bravest thing you can say

The bravest thing you can say.
Is not a speech or a shout.
It's not "I'm fine"
When the voices are loud.
The bravest thing you can say.
Is one small word.
Help.
It's not a whisper of weakness,
Not a crack in the wall.
It's a hand reaching out.
To catch you when you fall.
It takes a heart full of courage.
To speak when you're low.
To say, "I can't do this alone,"
And let someone know.
Because asking for help.
Is a step through the flame.
It's standing up.
And saying your name.
It's brave to be honest.
It's strong to be true.
It's bold to admit.
What you're going through.
So if you're hurting.
Please don't delay.
The bravest thing you can say
Is simply help.
And that's okay.

I didn't think it would work

I sat in the chair, not sure what to say.
They said EMDR could help in some way.
"Hold these buzzers one in each hand"
"And watch the light move, just like we planned."
The light moved left, then right, then back.
My hands buzzed gently, click, clack, click, clack.
I thought of old things, things I still lack.
But slowly, the weight began to crack.
The pain came up, but it didn't stay.
Bit by bit, it faded away.
At first, I thought it was kind of strange.
How could this help my life to change?
But slowly I started to feel more free.
Like something heavy was leaving me.
It didn't erase what happened before.
But it doesn't hurt me anymore.
I feel more calm, more safe, more strong.
This is what I've been wanting all along.
I didn't think it would help at the start.
But now I feel lighter inside my heart.
EMDR helped me in ways I didn't expect.
And gave me some peace, some self-respect.
It helped me learn to forgive myself.
And really improved my mental health.
I am shocked by the way that it works.
There was a time I didn't think things could get worse.
But I was surprised and things improved.
All those negative emotions have been moved.
No more flashbacks in the middle of the day.
No more nightmares chasing me away.
I can now have a good and restful sleep.
My past no longer cuts so deep.
I still remember, and that's okay.
But it doesn't control me every day.

I live my life, I laugh and grow.
There's peace inside me now, I know.
EMDR gave me space to heal.
And showed me that healing from trauma is real.

Understanding

It's not always the doctors.
Not always the staff.
Who catches me when I'm falling.
Who helped me find my laugh.
It's the ones down the hallway.
In rooms just like mine.
Who knows how it feels.
To not always feel fine.
We talk late at night.
Or sit side by side.
They are always there for me.
Even when I've cried.
We're all different here.
But we share something true.
They understand me.
In a way others can't do.
They know what it's like.
To feel lost or low.
They've been through the struggles.
And help me to grow.
The staff try their best.
But they don't always see.
What it means to be patient.
Like the others do with me.
Through the hard days and nights.
They've got my back.
They understand me.
When nothing else does.
And that's what I lack.
We share our struggles.
We share our pain.
But with each other.
We feel less strain.
The time slips away.

When we're lost in the fun.
A game for a distraction.
Until the day is done.
We're more than just patients.
We're friends who hold tight.
In a place that feels dark.
We bring each other light.

Things might look differently, but it can still be something great

Things in life don't always go the way we expected.
But we need to understand that things can't always be perfected.
Life can get in the way and we may end up on a different road.
But don't give up and stay in your determined mode.
Because believe me you can make something
great out of a shit situation.
As long as you have hope in your heart
and don't lose your determination.
Something that seems so broken can be put back
together, it will just look a little different.
But you can still do something so magnificent.
My life didn't go the way I thought it would.
But I still grasped all the opportunities I could so I could grow.
Five years ago, I would have pictured a
very, very different life for myself.
But things can get in the way, such as my mental health.
My road looks very different from what I had planned.
But even though it's different it can still be great
and that's what I want people to understand.
Where I am now was never part of my plan.
But at the same time it feels like my journey has just began.
I'm excited for the future and if this is how much my life can
change within a year, imagine what can happen in another year.
There are so many opportunities around me.
So just because it's not what I expected, it can still be great.
And always remember, it is never ever too late.

My biggest fear

When it comes to the topic of my biggest fear.
You'd expect me to say something like heights
or spiders, something severe.
But that is actually not the real truth.
You see, I've been struggling with my mental health since my youth.
And my biggest fear is the thought that I'll never get better.
And that one day I'll have to start writing my letter.
I can't bear the thought of my life to always be about suffering.
When what I really need and want is to start recovering.
But I fear I will always be sad.
And I'll always, always feel bad.
I'll always be the girl who self-harms.
I'll always be the girl with cuts and burns on her arms.
I'll always be the girl that is mentally ill.
I'll fear I'll always have this pain in my head and it will kill.
I ask myself every single day will I ever recover.
But at the end of the day that's something I'll have discovered.
And I can only hope that one day I look back
and I will be in shock I ever felt that way.
But I won't know if that day comes, until it's that day.
So until then, all I can do now is fight.
And pray and hope that one day, I will see the light.

Mental health awareness month

Last year I wrote a little rhyme.
To share a thought and to take the time.
It was for May Mental Health Awareness Month.
A time to talk, a time for truth.
And now it's here again this year.
The message stays, but let's be clear.
It's not just one month we should care.
Mental health is always there.
It's more common than we show.
More people hurt than we might know.
It doesn't care how old you are.
Where you're from, or who you are.
Any race, any gender.
Any background, soft or tender.
Anyone can feel the weight.
And sometimes help arrives too late.
The system needs to grow and mend.
More support we must defend.
We need more voices, open hearts.
This is where the healing starts.
Don't bottle up what's deep inside.
You don't have to run, you don't have to hide.
Speak your truth, be proud, be loud.
There's strength in standing with the crowd.
The stigma hurts, it makes us small.
But breaking it can help us all.
So let's keep talking, let's be brave.
Every story helps to pave.
A world that listens, learns, and lifts.
Where care and kindness are the gifts.

This month we speak, but let's agree.
Mental health should always be free.
Not just today, not just this May.
But every single kind of day.

My liver took what my heart couldn't handle

My liver took what my heart couldn't handle.
Is something I often like to say.
Because I don't drink for the taste.
But because it helps me get through the day.
Alcohol changes the way that I feel.
Which is why I choose to drink.
But it doesn't change the fact these emotions are real.
And it changes the way I think.
When I'm under the influence everything is easier.
It makes my emotions go away.
But they don't go away forever.
They always come back at the end of the day.
When I drink I feel more confident, I feel on top of the world.
I feel like a brand new person.
But I know this feeling won't last.
It will only make my mental health worsen.
I need to get better at feeling rather than numbing.
Because the drink helps me numb.
But I need to face them and stop running.
Because that's the thing that needs to be done.
Drinking doesn't make my problems go away.
Nor does it make them disappear.
It just pushes them further.
But they are still very near.
I find most people drink because there is something going on inside.
Something going on inside their heart.
So they drink, drink and drink to hide.
Till them and their emotions are far apart.
So my liver takes everything I can't take.
But that's not the way to do things.
Because this is a big, big mistake.
You will get stuck in this vicious cycle.

So feel your emotions, speak about what's going on in your head.
And stop drinking to change the way you feel.
It's better to face them head on instead.

Mood swings

One thing I hate about EUPD.
Is the mood wings that come with it you see.
We all get mood swings, right.
But in EUPD it's a different kind of fight.
My mood can swing in unpredictable ways.
And sometimes I wish this was just a phase.
My mood can go from one extreme to another.
It can happen anytime of the year, even in the summer.
I can go from being suicidal and not seeing a way out.
To feel on top of the world and wanting to shout.
And my mood swings confuse people because they are so fast.
And sometimes my emotions change so quickly they don't even last.
I become impulsive and don't think before I act.
I don't see that my actions can have a negative impact.
And then I am full of shame and regret.
And I feel so angry and upset.
I just wish my mood could be steady and stable.
I want to control my mood but I feel so unable.
I genuinely cannot control these extreme mood swings.
I never know what the next day is gonna bring.
Within one day my mood can switch so many times.
And it makes me wanna do something stupid sometimes.
The mood swings are the worst part about this condition.
And it's about time it gets some recognition.

The psych ward

I cannot stand being on this ward.
Wandering the halls lost and bored.
The psych ward is such a traumatic place to be.
I don't want to be here, I just want to be free.
When I'm struggling I get told to use my skills.
And if that doesn't work maybe some pills.
Being here often feels like a prison sentence.
Except I'm not a criminal and I don't need to show repentance.
I haven't done anything bad or anything wrong.
I'm doing what I can to be brave and strong.
But every minute here feels like an hour.
I feel I have no control and no power.
Like all my decisions are taken and I don't get a choice.
When I do have a say and I do have a voice
I struggle to just get to the end of the day.
I can't see a good ending or see a way.
I want to be home with my family and friends.
But this admission feels like it never ends.
Days turn into weeks that turn into months
and suddenly it's been a year.
I just want to leave. I really don't want to be here.
I've seen things I never wanted to see.
This is such a traumatic place to be.
The weekends last forever and feel so long.
Why do I feel this is a punishment like I've done something wrong?
All I want to do is go home, which is where I truly, truly belong.

My truth

My poetry isn't just my poetry.
I want people to see what I see.
My book isn't just my book.
I want the world to take a look.
Those verses aren't just verses that I choose to rhyme.
Writing these poems helped me in a really difficult time.
Those words aren't just words.
They are my truth that I want to be heard.
I know people may not agree.
But that's okay.
Because this is my truth.
And this is my way.

Rely

If there's anything I've learned in my 20 years of life.
Is that you can't rely on anyone to help you survive.
The system won't be there to catch you when you fall.
The crisis line won't always pick up when you try to call.
Your family and true friends will always stay.
But they can't make those demons in your head go away.
They can be there for you alongside.
But support and love is all they can provide.
You have to be the one to make the change.
And maybe some things in my life I need to rearrange.
The professionals said you're safe now with
white walls and plastic chairs.
Routine meals, pills, and staff who claim to care.
But behind each clipboard, I see it clear.
The system doesn't mend, it doesn't hear.
No law rewrites itself for me.
No policy sets my spirit free.
The forms get signed, the bed's reset.
And I walk out with no safety net.
I used to think they'd fix it all.
A hand to catch me when I fall.
But the truth is raw, and the truth is mine.
Only I can climb this spine.
Let them tick their discharge box.
I'll build my world from shattered rocks.
Not because the system sees.
But because I believe in me.

Nighttime on the ward

As soon as I lay down in my bed.
I am now alone with the thoughts inside my head.
I want to go to sleep but I am also scared.
Because on the ward you can never be prepared.
You never know what noises will wake you up in the night.
You never know when they'll turn on your light.
I've woken up to banging, screaming and the alarm.
And I struggle to remain steady and calm.
If you leave your room there is absolutely no one around.
It feels and looks like a ghost town.
I find I struggle more at night when I'm all alone.
So I just lie there in my bed on my phone.
Night times are scary on the ward.
Sitting alone, lost and bored.
I lay there waiting for the night to be gone and done.
I feel a lot better when it's the day and I can see the sun.

Breathe

Breathe they said.
Breathe with me instead.
One simple word.
That had to be heard.
Just take one minute and breathe.
And this feeling will leave.
Just like a storm it will eventually pass.
It will shatter just like glass.
When you breathe it's a reminder you are alive.
And you are in control and you will survive.
Just breathe with me.
And you will see.
That you can be set free.

Care

We all want someone to care.
Someone to say:
"I'm worried about you."
"I'm here."
"I've got you."
"It's okay."
"Breathe."
Not because we're weak.
But because we're human.
We weren't made to walk alone.
Not through pain.
Not through joy.
We need hands to hold.
Eyes that see.
Voices that soften the weight we carry.
It's not asking for too much.
It's not too much.
It's just the way we're built.
Hhearts needing other hearts.
To beat beside.
We all want someone to care.
And that's okay.
Really.
That's okay.

Surviving the sterile room

Sterile Room.
They said the words.
Sterile room.
And fear ran through me.
Like a fire I couldn't stop.
I cried.
I shouted, "I'm scared."
Because I was.
Because I don't do well with change.
That crashes in.
Without a warning.
There was nothing.
Not empty like peace.
But empty like punishment.
A bed.
A pillow.
A blanket.
Chair too heavy to lift.
A cup of water.
Toilet roll.
That's all.
No clothes.
No soap.
No book to hold.
No sound.
No comfort.
Just time.
And too much of it.
Twelve hours.
Not long.
But it felt like days.
It was always my biggest fear.
Being stripped of myself.
I wouldn't wish it on anyone.

And when they let me back
My room wasn't my room.
They'd turned it over.
My things touched,
Moved.
Judged.
My books, my clothes,
Not how I left them.
It wasn't home.
It wasn't safe.
It was mine.
But I no longer felt like it.
It was an invasion.
It was trauma.
And I'm still picking up the pieces.

I've seen it all

I've seen it all
From the quiet waiting rooms
With ticking clocks and too bright lights
To the chaos of A&E
Where screams echo down the halls
And time stands still
I've sat in corners
Holding back tears
While strangers whispered my fate
I've been locked behind heavy doors
With nothing but a pillow
A blanket
And fear
I've watched others break
Seen eyes lose their light
Heard stories that should never have to be told
I've seen hands tied down
Meds forced in
Freedom stripped
In the name of care
They say it's to help
They say it's for your own good
But I've seen the damage
The trauma it leaves behind
Wounds that don't show
But I bleed every day
I've seen people forgotten
I've felt what it's like
To be just another name
On just another file
To scream for help
And hear silence back
I'm just one of thousands
Trapped in the cracks

Held by a system
Meant to heal
But sometimes it causes harm
We carry scars that no one sees
And stories no one wants to hear
But I'll still speak
We all should
Because change only comes
When someone dares to say
I've seen it all
And it cannot stay this way
I've seen things I cannot unsee
And these things will forever traumatise me.

Time

Time
In the psych ward, time stands still
Each tick of the clock is a test of my will
A minute crawls like a heavy stone
You feel it deep, down to the bone
An hour stretches, long and wide
Like waves that never touched the tide
A single day feels far too steep
No rest, no peace, not even sleep
A week drags on, slow and thick
Each moment playing the same old trick
A month becomes a mountain tall
You climb and climb but always fall
And months turn into endless years
Built from silence, meds, and tears
So much time just fades away
Wasted thoughts and shades of grey
Time isn't ours to throw or keep
It's not a toy, it runs so deep
It's precious, priceless, thin as air
But here, it just isn't fair
We wait, we sit, we try to heal
While time forgets how to feel
Outside it flies, in here it crawls
A shadow trapped between four walls.

More

I am more
Than what I am in here for
I am more
Then all the things I've done before
I'm more than a name on a chart
More than a label pulled apart
I'm more than pills on a silver tray
More than the dark thoughts that won't go away
I'm more than a bed and a ticking clock
More than the stares when I try to talk
I'm more than a moment where I broke
More than the words I never spoke
I'm more than a scream or a silent cry
More than the days I wanted to die
I'm more than the lows that pull me down
More than the silence when no one's around
I'm more than the weight I carry inside
More than the secrets I try to hide
I'm more than a file, a code, a case
More than the tears that pour down my face
I breathe and fight
And flame
I still am
Despite the name
I am more
Than what I'm in here for
I'm more than the things I've done before
I'm more
I'm more
I'm more.

It's not my drinking,
it's my thinking

It's not the bottle
or the glass in my hand
it's the thought that whispers
"you won't cope", " you won't stand"
it's not the drink
that pulls me in deep
it's the ache in my chest
when I try just to sleep
it's the loop in my mind
that says "just one more"
like that will fix
what I can't ignore
I don't drink for the taste
or the buzz, or the fun
I drink to escape
what I can't outrun
the fear, the shame
the silent fight
the way my thoughts
keep me up at night
addiction wears
a thousand masks
drugs, food, phones
so many tasks
but under it all
the pain's the same
a mind that burns
a heart in chains
we all reach out
for something to cope
but what we need
is a thread of hope

not to silence
or numb or hide
but to sit with the storm
and not run inside
it's not my drinking
that needs to mend
it's the way I think
I don't want to pretend
it's the same mindset
just different things
but being honest
is where recovery begins
so don't just treat
what's in my hand
help me face
what I don't understand.

It kept me safe, but it didn't keep me sane

They locked the doors
and took my phone
said I'd be safe
but I felt alone.
White walls and silence
then screams in the night
nurses with needles
too tired to fight.
They called it help
but it felt like a cage
each hour that passed
just filled me with rage.
I saw too much
things I can't unsee
pain in the faces
of people like me.
Cried in the corner
afraid of the sound
of someone next door
being held to the ground.
I wasn't a danger
just lost and afraid
but the ward turned my fear
into memories that stayed.
Now I flinch at the quiet
I freeze at the loud
I carry the weight
and that is allowed.
It kept me breathing
but it broke my mind
left me with ghosts
I can't leave behind.

So yes, I lived
but not the same
it kept me safe
but not my brain.

Expert by experience

I would consider myself to be an expert in mental health
Not because I had good grades
Or a fancy degree
But because I see what others don't see
I've been where you are
At absolutely my worst time
And I understand what it's like
Because it's a mountain I had to climb
I'm an expert strictly from experience
And my experience one and only
Because I know what it's like to feel sad
Depressed, anxious, even lonely
When people think of an expert in
something they think qualifications
But that's not always the most valuable part
It's the people who understand what it's like
What it's like to have a heavy heart
And I want to use my experience to help others like me
So my experience wasn't all for nothing
An awful situation turned into something amazing
And all this suffering, turned into something
Now I sit with others in their silence and pain
Not to fix them just to stay in the rain
To say, "You're not broken, you're just worn thin
And healing's not easy, but it can begin."
I speak the language of panic and doubt
Of days when you whisper, "I want to get out."
But I also know moments when light filters through
And slowly, so slowly, you start to feel you
It's not something textbooks could ever have shown
How to hold someone else when they feel all alone
But I've lived it, I've felt it, I've broken, I've bled
And I've stitched up my soul with words left unsaid
So if you're struggling, please know this is true

You're not weak, you're just doing what humans do
And though I don't have letters after my name
I've walked through the fire, and I'm not the same
I'm an expert by experience raw, real, and true
And if you need someone, I'll sit here with you
Because sometimes the greatest wisdom we share
Is simply to say: "I've been there. I care."
Experience is priceless, no money could buy
The lessons you learn when you're just getting by
It's carved in the moments that tore me apart
Now those same moments help me open my heart.

We need to change the words

They say "sterile room" but that sounds so cold
Like I'm somewhere forgotten, not someone to hold
They say, "we'll IM you" or "we'll inject",
And suddenly care feels more like neglect.
They label us "psychotic", "paranoid", "not well",
As if we are problems, as if we can't tell
"Agitated," "non-compliant", those words sting
When really, we're just trying to survive everything
These words are sharp, they cut like a blade
And in those moments, we feel afraid.
We need to change the way we speak,
To lift up the broken, empower the weak.
Because language can comfort or language can harm
It can either cause panic or bring calm
A softer word, a gentler tone
Can turn a ward into something like home.
They used to say "lunatic bin", "nut house", "mad",
Words soaked in stigma, cruel and sad.
Back in the day: "insane asylum" they'd shout,
But all that did was shut people out
Now we say mental health hospital and that's a start,
But we must treat it like any other part
Of our healthcare system, with dignity and care,
Because mental or physical, it's all still there.
The words we use shape how people heal,
They shape how we're treated, how we feel.
I'm not a case, or a file on a chart
I'm a human being, with a voice and a heart.
So let's change the words, remove the fear,
Make compassion louder, make respect clear.
Because as someone who's lived this, I truly believe
With different words, we help people breathe.

Missing out

There is so much I'm missing out on by being in hospital
I could be on holiday somewhere sunny and tropical
I'm missing out on life changing opportunities like education
And I'm stuck in what feels like an impossible situation
How can there be a good ending to this chapter of my life
I'm missing out on working, having kids, becoming a wife
The time I've spent here I will never ever get back
I really need to get out of here and get back on track
I wanna go out with my friends clubbing and drinking
But instead I'm in this hospital room alone and thinking
I miss the feeling of fresh air and the wind in my hair
Instead, I'm breathing stale silence and hospital care
I should be making memories, laughing until I cry
Not lying in this bed, watching days pass me by
My phone lights up with pictures from people outside
While I sit here, trying to swallow my pride
I miss the noise, the chaos, the sound of the street
Not the echo of footsteps and nurses' feet
There's so much I want to do, so much I want to see
But it all feels out of reach, so far away from me
They say healing takes time, but it's stealing mine too
And I'm scared of the future, not knowing what I'll do
But deep down I'm hoping, though it's hidden by pain
That I'll find my way out, and feel like me again.

The mask

We might wear a smile to cover the pain
Pretending we're okay again and again
Sometimes we laugh, join in with the crowd
But inside our thoughts are screaming loud
It's hard to explain what we're going through
Especially when no one has a clue
So please be gentle, patient and kind
You never know what's going on in someone's mind
Not every wound is something you can see
But kindness and care can help set us free
The mask we wear helps us survive
But behind it, we're barely alive
We hide our struggles, we hide the tears
We've bottled up pain for so many years
So look past the surface, don't just assume
That someone's okay because they light up the room
Behind every smile might be a plea
To be noticed, supported, and simply set free
So next time you ask if someone's alright
Listen with your heart, hold their pain light
Because the mask is heavy, the silence is loud
And anyone can struggle, it is allowed.

Privacy and dignity

When you walk on to the ward
You leave your dignity at the door
When you walk onto the ward
Your privacy is now ignored
They can search through all your things
Your letters, drawings, memories, rings
They take away what makes you "you"
And say it's all for safety too
They knock but don't wait for a reply
They come in even when you cry
There's nowhere safe to just be still
You lose your say, you lose your will
Even when you're trying to sleep
They shine a torch, they come and peek
You're never really on your own
Even bathrooms feel not like home
You're not treated like you're grown
You're watched, you're followed but you still feel alone
It's hard to heal when every day
Parts of yourself are stripped away.

Glorified

Psych hospitals are glorified online
But people who are in these places are not just fine
Patients lose their lives when staff didn't see the signs
The alarms are now drilled into my head
They wake me up in the middle of the night when I am in bed
I wish I could be home with my family instead
You hear patients banging their head on the wall
Someone pacing up and down the hall
Hearing staff press their emergency call
These places are not nice places to be
These places have really traumatised me
Because I've seen things I never wanted to see
You don't see what goes behind the walls of a psych ward
Patients wander the corridors alone and bored
Asking for help and support but they get ignored
They tell us it's help, they say it's care,
But half the time, it feels unfair
You're watched while you sleep, you're watched when you cry
And if you break down, they don't ask why
You're judged for the way you cope with pain
Treated like you're wild or insane
But no one chooses to end up here
We're just people lost in pain and fear
You learn to stay quiet, not make a fuss
Because speaking up feels dangerous
So many rules, so little grace
You start to feel like a disgrace
The food is cold, the lights too bright
You're trapped indoors day and night
No fresh air, no sense of time
Just meds and checklists and the same old line
I've watched friends break and not come back
While staff stay silent, keeping track
Of risk and charts and things to do

But forget that we are people too
So next time you hear how psych wards "heal"
Please ask someone how it really feels
Because it's not like the shows on TV
It's a fight to survive, not a place to be free
I worry that I won't make it out of here alive
Because truth be told I'm just trying to survive
This hospital could easily be the death of me
Which is why I need to be set free
This hospital has broke me and tried to put me back together
But the memories and the things I've seen
here will stay in my head forever
I've seen it all, I've heard it all, all what goes on behind these doors

What I'm known for

I am so much more
Than just another number on that door.
I am so much more
Than the meds I take,
Even if I feel I'm going to break.
I'm so much more than all my admissions.
I am so much more than my mental health conditions.
These diagnoses can feel like a prison sentence that is hell,
Stuck behind the walls of a place where we are unwell.
People walk past me in the street while I'm out on leave,
And they would find the truth hard to believe.
You would never guess I am sectioned in hospital
Behind my smile, it's sometimes unbearable.
I laugh at the bus stop, I chat on my phone,
But inside I carry battles I've fought on my own.
They see the outside, the clothes, the grin,
Not the storms I weather daily within.
They don't see the nights when I silently cry,
Or the mornings I wake just wishing to die.
But I am not weak, I'm fighting each day,
In ways most can't see, or begin to say.
I'm learning to breathe when panic takes hold,
I'm daring to heal, I'm trying to be bold.

Power

I feel all my decisions have been taken away
And I no longer get my opinion and my say,
I feel like massive life decisions are being made for me
But being able to have my say is really key.
I feel I am no longer living my life for myself
Because I am the priority and my mental health.
I just want to feel seen and I just want to feel heard,
I just want to be able to say what I would have preferred.
But somewhere along the line, I lost control,
Like I'm here in body, but not quite whole.
They tell me it's for the best, they say, "You'll see"
But I just want someone to listen to me.
I want to be asked, not just told what to do,
To be treated like a person, not something to get through.
It's hard to keep hope when choice disappears,
When your voice gets drowned out by professional fears.
I'm not just a risk or a case to assess
I'm a person in pain, trying my best.
Let me be part of the life I still own,
Don't leave me to face this all alone.
Because healing means more than meds and rest,
It means being heard and being seen as I wrestle this mess.
So let me speak, let me stand, let me try,
Don't make every choice for me while I watch life pass by.
I may be struggling, but I'm still me
Still worthy of dignity, still longing to be free.
Kewstoke before and after
It's the day before Kewstoke and I am so, so nervous
But I want to be there and have my purpose.
I'm reading a poem and playing the ukulele,
I've been preparing and practising so much lately.
I'm scared to do these things in front of a big crowd
But I have do it because I know after I will be so, so proud.
I'm scared my words will stutter or my hands will shake.

What if I mess up or even make a mistake?
I need to remember to keep going and go slow and steady,
I'm just not sure if I can do this, I don't feel ready.
But if I don't do this I will be full of regret,
I want this to be a good day I will never forget.
But what if I shine, even just a little light?
What if my voice brings someone strength tonight?
What if my hands, though shaky with fear,
Still strum a tune someone needed to hear?
I've come so far from where I began,
With every small step, I've proved that I can.
So I'll breathe in deep and stand up tall,
Even if my voice cracks, I'll give it my all.
This isn't about perfect, or getting it right,
It's about being brave in the face of the fright.
And when it's done, I'll know in my heart
I showed up, spoke out, and played my part.

After

So the day is over and Kewstoke is done
We had such a great time and so much fun
So many amazing people who shared their talents and skills
With laughter and music that gave us all chills
I stood there shaking, my heart beating fast
But I took a deep breath and faced it at last
With my uke in my hands and my poems to read
I gave it my all, I planted the seed
And oh, how it bloomed in the warmth of the crowd
Their smiles were gentle, their claps were loud
The nerves that once gripped me just melted away
And pride filled my chest by the end of the day
I was brave, I was present, I stood in my light
I felt so alive it all just felt right
I walked off that stage with my head held high
No longer afraid, just ready to fly

A day to remember, a moment to keep
That'll visit my heart when doubts start to creep
Kewstoke, you showed me what courage can do
And now I believe I'm proud to be me, too.

Mental health awareness day

Today is Mental health awareness day
And there are a few things I'd like to say
I never really understood the importance of mental health
Until it happened to me myself
It is so important to take care of our mental wellbeing
Telling someone how you feel can be so freeing
So many people suffer, more than we might know
Because many of us hide it and don't let it show
A simple question like "are you okay"
Could be the reason someone smiles today
a simple phrase like "I'm here for you"
Could help someone when they're feeling blue
And when someone says something like "I'm fine"
Take it with caution, it could be a sign
Many times I say I'm fine and walk away
But deep down part of me wanted to stay
But I just couldn't find the words to describe
Describe what I feel on the inside
My pain is too hard to explain
I feel I repeat myself again and again
Sometimes there's an obvious cause
Sometimes it's just a chemical imbalance in our brain
Our mind is a vital organ that needs attention
For conditions like bipolar, anxiety and depression
And the list goes on and they all deserve care
And if you don't quite understand I can make you aware
Because there was a time I didn't have a clue
What it meant to suffer and that is so true
But I have the experience and I understand what it's like
To spend months on end stuck in psych
To be stripped from myself
And to be judged for my mental health
I understand the feeling of wanting to take your last breath
and when you wake up, you're disappointed you escaped death

I know what's it like to be let down by a system that is meant to heal
I know what's it's like to be judged for the way you feel
I've faced the stigma, I've put up with stares
I know the pain of believing no one cares
while I wish I could take my own pain away
It's part of the reason I am who I am today
And I want to move to a better place on this earth
A place where even if you're struggling you know your worth
We need to come together and unite as one
Because believe me when I say, mental health can happen to anyone
The stigma needs to be broken
And we need to be more open
We need to educate those who might know
What it's like to struggle, what it's like to feel low
Because it's one in four of us who will experience mental health
So if it's not you yourself
It could be someone you love
But it's also a time to remember those up above
Because just like any part of the body, this can kill
And change won't come if we just stay silent and still
We need to encourage people to reach out when things are hard
And the one thing we must not do, is disregard
Prioritise your mental health just like
you would your physical health
Mental health can affect anyone, regardless
of age, background or gender
Mental needs to be at the core and be at the centre
Of everything we do, mental health always comes first
Because if we ignore it things will only get worse
So let's stand up and let's stand together
Because I do believe things can get better
Let's speak about our pain
With absolutely no shame
Let's stand up and let's say our name
Let's destroy that stigma because we are not to blame

To end this rhyme
Let's just take the time
To appreciate and understand the importance of today
For mental health awareness day
It's so much more than just a day highlighted in the calendar
Because mental health awareness should always matter
It's not just important for one single day
Because mental health doesn't just go away
Just because it's a certain time of year
Doesn't mean our mental health disappears
Mental health is always here
Not just for one day, but all 365 days of the year.

Acknowledgements

I would like to dedicate this book to my beloved niece, Star, who sadly isn't here today to see me publish my second book; however, I know she would be very proud. Anytime I look into the sky and see a star, I will always remember you, I love you, Star.

I would also like to thank all the people who have sponsored me and helped me to get this book published, without you, it wouldn't be possible.

I want to thank one of my best friends Resa who lives all the way in America, but despite being very far away she never fails to be there for me when I need her.

Once again I want to thank my amazing support worker Cha, who always offers me consistency and support without a fail. And has been one of my biggest supports along this journey.

Last but not least, I want to say a very big thank you to all the team from UK Book Publishing. They have been very supportive and understanding when working with me. In addition they made the process very straightforward.

www.ingramcontent.com/pod-product-compliance
Lightning Source LLC
Chambersburg PA
CBHW070811050426
42452CB00011B/1995